GOOD FOOD
FAST
FAY MASCHLER

NOTE

1. All recipes serve four unless otherwise stated.

2. All spoon measurements are level. Spoon measures can be bought in both imperial and metric sizes to give accurate measurement of small quantities.

3. All eggs are size 2 or 3 unless otherwise stated.

4. All sugar is granulated unless otherwise stated.

5. Preparation times are an average calculated during recipe testing.

6. Metric and imperial measurements have been calculated separately. Use one set of measurements only as they are not exact equivalents.

7. Cooking times may vary slightly depending on the individual oven. Dishes should be placed in the centre of an oven unless otherwise specified.

8. Always preheat the oven or grill to the specified temperature.

9. If using a fan-assisted oven, follow the manufacturer's instructions for guidance on temperature adjustments.

First published in this edition by
The Octopus Publishing Group
Michelin House, 81 Fulham Road, London SW3 6RB

Some of these recipes previously appeared in
Eating In, published by Bloomsbury 1987

ISBN 0 86273 4746

Printed in Italy

SOUPS AND STARTERS

It is the ingredients, rather than the methods used, which transform these soups and starters from the mundane to the sublime. All that is needed is a touch more creativity in the supermarket. Jerusalem artichokes make the superb Palestine Soup, Stilton Tartlets have the edge over quiche, while it's the wise chef who tries Confucius Salad.

Green minestrone

AVGOLEMONO

1.2 litres (2 pints) chicken stock
salt
freshly ground black pepper
1 heaped tablespoon rice (or meatballs)
2 eggs
juice of 1 lemon

Meatballs
225 g (8 oz) minced veal or lamb
2 tablespoons fresh white breadcrumbs
1 onion, peeled and finely chopped
1 teaspoon chopped fresh dill or parsley
1 small egg (size 5)
salt
freshly ground pepper

Preparation time: 10–20 minutes
Cooking time: 30–40 minutes

In a village that I like in Greece, there used to be holiday villas for parties of English people staffed by jolly, upper-middle-class English girls. I remember listening to one of them as a local restaurateur attempted to convince her that this was the right place to bring the guests on the girl's night off. He reeled off the predictable list of specialities: moussaka, souvlaki, garides, bresaola, biftecki, and so on.

'Oh super!' cried the girl.

'Yes,' he said in Greek, anxious to meet her demands, *'ke soupa.'*

This is perhaps the most typical Greek soupa. Using the same technique, but with less stock or liquid, you can make egg and lemon sauce, ideal for chicken, fish, meatballs or poached vegetables.

1. Heat the stock and check for seasoning. Add the rice and cook until tender.
2. In a small bowl, beat together the eggs and lemon juice. Add a small cup of the stock to the egg and lemon and beat it in. Return this to the pan, whisking with a balloon whisk or similar over a low heat, until the soup is slightly thickened. Do not let it boil or the egg will curdle.
3. You can add meatballs as follows, omitting the rice. Mix together very thoroughly the ingredients for the meatballs. Form into small balls. Poach them in the chicken stock for 15 minutes. Remove the meatballs with a slotted spoon and place in a heated dish. Proceed with the egg and lemon method as above. Pour over the meatballs and serve.

POTAGE BONNE FEMME

2 large leeks or 3–4 skinny ones
40 g (1½ oz) butter
225 g (8 oz) carrots, peeled and diced
450 g (1 lb) potatoes, peeled and diced
1.2 litres (2 pints) water
salt
freshly ground black pepper
a pinch of white or brown sugar
1 tablespoon finely chopped parsley
50 ml (2 fl oz) double cream (optional)

Preparation time: about 10 minutes
Cooking time: about 30 minutes
Microwave time: 23 minutes

This is one of the least expensive soups to make, but also one of the most satisfying.

In France the ingredients are sometimes not puréed in a blender or even pushed through a mouli-légumes – the potatoes are just crushed against the side of the pan – but most people find an emulsion more appetizing.

1. Clean the leeks very thoroughly. To do this, trim them top and bottom, leaving a considerable amount of the dark green part intact. Slice through the dark green part with a sharp knife, so that in washing the leeks you can check that all the grit is removed from between the layers of leaves. Shake the leaves dry and slice them.
2. Melt the butter in a large pan and, when it is beginning to froth, add the prepared leeks and carrots. Let them become glistening with butter and thoroughly hot.
3. Add the prepared potatoes, water, a little salt, pepper and sugar. Simmer for about 30 minutes.
4. Whizz in a blender or food processor, or put through the mouli-légumes. Return to the pan. Check for seasoning and add the parsley and the cream, if you are using it.
5. Serve in warmed bowls with hot French bread.

MICROWAVE
Place butter in a bowl and cook on Full (100%) power for 1 minute. Add the sliced leeks and diced carrots, cover and cook on Full (100%) power for 6 minutes, stirring once. Add the diced potatoes, half the water, a little salt, pepper and sugar. Cover. Cook on Full (100%) power for 12–14 minutes, stirring once. Blend as in step 4 and add cream. Reheat on Full (100%) power for 2 minutes.

FAR RIGHT: Avgolemono
RIGHT: Potage bonne femme

GREEN MINESTRONE

SERVES 4–6
225 g (8 oz) fresh broad beans
225 g (8 oz) fresh peas in their pods
225 g (8 oz) asparagus, tips reserved
225 g (8 oz) broccoli
a chunk of cauliflower
1 bunch spring onions, trimmed and peeled
2 garlic cloves, peeled and chopped
225 g (8 oz) French green beans
25 g (1 oz) butter
4 tablespoons virgin olive oil
salt
freshly ground black pepper
75 g (3 oz) Parmesan cheese, freshly grated

Preparation time: about 20 minutes
Cooking time: about 25 minutes

I like this minestrone with a visible sheen of Tuscan olive oil on top. Freshly grated Parmesan cheese is another important detail. The vegetables listed above are a guideline. Some can be omitted, others added. The hearts of globe artichokes, for example, are lovely.

1. Prepare all the vegetables, shelling the broad beans and peas, cleaning and chopping the rest into quite small pieces.
2. Heat the butter and half the olive oil in a large, heavy-bottomed sauté pan. Add the asparagus stalks (saving the tips for later), the broccoli, cauliflower, spring onions, garlic and green and broad beans. Toss them in the fat until glistening and beginning to soften. Add the peas.
3. Add just enough water to cover and season with salt and pepper. Cook gently until the vegetables are tender, but still crunchy, then turn off the heat.
4. Remove half the vegetables and whizz in a food processor or liquidizer until you have a none too smooth purée. Pour into a clean pan and bring to the simmer, adding more water if you want a thinner consistency.
5. Add the reserved vegetables plus the asparagus tips. Stir and heat through. Taste for seasoning and for texture.
6. Take off the heat. Serve in shallow plates with a trickle of oil on top and the Parmesan cheese handed separately.

STILTON TARTLETS

40 g (1½ oz) butter
1 large onion peeled and sliced
100 g (4 oz) Stilton cheese
3 eggs
300 ml (½ pint) double cream
salt
freshly ground black pepper
2 tomatoes, peeled and sliced

Shortcrust Pastry:
225 g (8 oz) plain flour
1 teaspoon dry mustard powder
a pinch of salt
1 teaspoon dried oregano
50 g (2 oz) butter
50 g (2 oz) lard
about 2 tablespoons ice-cold water

Preparation time: about 25 minutes, plus resting
Cooking time: about 1 hour
Oven: 180°C, 350°F, Gas Mark 4, then 160°C, 325°F, Gas Mark 3

Most blue cheeses would work well in the recipe. The dried oregano in the shortcrust pastry is a good ruse. To save time, make the pastry the day before, wrap in clingfilm and chill in the refrigerator.

1. Make the pastry by sifting the flour with the mustard and a pinch of salt. Add the oregano. Rub in the fats until the mixture resembles breadcrumbs.
2. Add the ice-cold water and mix, first with a knife and then with one hand. It might be necessary to add a little more water but don't overdo it or the pastry will be tough; add only enough water, really, to make it cohere. Let it rest, if possible, for 30 minutes wrapped in clingfilm.
3. Roll out the pastry and line small tartlet pans or, should you have no suitable container, make one larger tart.
4. Cover with foil and dried beans and bake 'blind' for 20 minutes. Remove the pastry and lower the oven temperature.
5. Melt the butter and cook the onion gently until softened. Chop the Stilton roughly and add to the pan. Cook until melted. Quite a lot of oil will separate. Pour this away.
6. Beat the eggs with the cream and season with salt and pepper. When the onion and cheese mixture has cooled a little, stir it in.
7. Divide the mixture between the tartlet cases or pour it into the one case. Place a slice of tomato on each tart, or arrange the slices over the large tart, and bake for 30 minutes until golden brown. Serve with a little salad as a first course.

ABOVE LEFT: Green minestrone
BELOW LEFT: Stilton tartlets

PALESTINE SOUP

450 g (1 lb) Jerusalem artichokes
salt
1 large onion, peeled and chopped
½ celery stick, chopped
100 g (4 oz) butter
1 garlic clove, peeled and chopped
2 bacon rashers, chopped
1 litre (1¾ pints) chicken stock or water
250 ml (8 fl oz) top of the milk, milk or thin cream
freshly ground black pepper
2 tablespoons toasted shelled hazelnuts, coarsely ground or finely chopped

Preparation time: about 20 minutes
Cooking time: about 25 minutes

Some say Jerusalem artichokes are so called because when they came to this country in the early seventeenth century, botanists recognized that they were girasols, plants whose flowers turn with the sun; from girasol it is not too far to Jerusalem and hence Palestine Soup. The French name, topinambour, is just as interesting: since the vegetable arrived in France at the same time as a number of Brazilian Tupi Tambo Indians, it got labelled with the same name. This vegetable has a marvellous subtle flavour. It was Escoffier who thought of the felicitous combination of toasted hazelnuts with pureed artichokes.

1. Trim, wash and boil the artichokes in salted water for about 7 minutes, then plunge them into cold water and take off the peel. Alternatively, peel them raw if they are not too knobbly.
2. Chop them into dice. Gently cook them with the onion and celery in half the butter, stirring occasionally, for 5 minutes.
3. Add the garlic, bacon and stock or water. Simmer until all is tender.
4. Either liquidize, whizz in a food processor or push through a mouli-légumes. Add the milk or cream and check for seasoning.
5. Stir in the remaining butter and pour into a tureen or individual bowls. Scatter the nuts on top.

FRIED AUBERGINES WITH SKORDALIA

1 large or 2 medium aubergines
salt
4 plump garlic cloves
1 fat slice stale white bread
75 g (3 oz) ground almonds
150 ml (¼ pint) olive oil
freshly ground black pepper
lemon juice
seasoned plain flour
more olive oil or vegetable oil, for frying

Preparation time: about 35 minutes
Cooking time: about 15–20 minutes

I first tasted aubergines cooked in one of the ways I like them best in the house of a Greek friend: sliced, floured, fried and served with a garlicky sauce called Skordalia. Mrs Karayiannis, the Greek woman who made them, had been very keen to own a Kenwood mixer so I had valiantly carried one, plus attachments, from London where they were alleged to be cheaper. She used it once for this sauce – generally made with a good deal of laborious pounding – washed it, carefully wrapped it in plastic and put it in to a cupboard. I think it is sometimes paraded for friends.

1. Aubergine slices must be salted and left to bead with perspiration to remove bitterness and to stop them mopping up quantities of oil. Cut into 5 mm (¼ inch) slices. Lay in a colander and sprinkle with salt.
2. Unlike Mrs Karayiannis you will probably want to use a blender or food processor rather than pestle and mortar for the sauce. Peel and crush the garlic cloves. Trim the bread of crusts, soak the crumb in water and squeeze it tightly in your hand. Put the garlic and bread into the food processor for a brief whizz. Add the almonds and blend.
3. Slowly add the olive oil, as if for mayonnaise, until you have a homogeneous thick sauce. Season with salt, pepper and lemon juice to taste. If it looks a bit porridgy, the texture and colour can be improved with a little milk or thin cream. Pile into a bowl.
4. With kitchen paper wipe the aubergines. Shake them in a bag with seasoned flour. Heat the oil to the depth of about 5 mm (¼ inch) in a frying pan. Vegetable oil can be used for economy.
5. Fry the aubergine slices, turning them once, until golden. Drain on kitchen paper. You will have to do batches, keeping them warm the while. Serve immediately with the skordalia sauce.

ABOVE RIGHT: Palestine soup
BELOW RIGHT: Fried aubergines with skordalia

PEASE SOUP

1 large onion, peeled and sliced
1 tablespoon oil
1 teaspoon coriander seeds
1 teaspoon cumin seeds
1 fresh green chilli pepper
garlic, to taste
1 × 400 g (14 oz) can pease pudding
few cupfuls of boiling water
salt
freshly ground black pepper
slivers of green chilli, to garnish

Preparation time: about 10 minutes
Cooking time: 15–20 minutes

Finding a can of pease pudding in my local supermarket reminded me of an interview I once did with the journalist Michael Bateman on the subject of his approach to cooking. He was very good on the business of getting something quickly on to the table after returning from work. The recipe below I tried to write in his style of delivery.

1. We assume you have just come home from work. Nothing is ready to eat. Before you take off your hat and coat, peel and slice an onion, making long strips, and set it to fry in a little oil in a heavy frying pan. Let it brown. Let it burn. You want it slippery; part sweet, part charred, caramelized. This is a reckless recipe.
2. Throw in crushed coriander seeds and cumin seeds, the chilli pepper, finely chopped (include the seeds), and as much chopped garlic as you want. Mix it round aggressively.
3. Spoon in the pease pudding – it will catch and burn a bit. Stir. Pour in a few cupfuls of boiling water. Scrape around the pan to release the flavours.
4. Turn it all into a saucepan. Thin to the desired consistency with more water. Season with Maldon salt and freshly ground black pepper. Garnish with slivers of green chilli.

WALNUT, BEETROOT AND CHICORY SALAD

2 plump heads of chicory
100 g (¼ lb) lamb's lettuce (sometimes called corn salad or mâche) or frisée (curly endive) if you can find them
2 large cooked beetroot
175 g (6 oz) 'wet' walnuts in their shells
1 crisp eating apple (optional variation)

Vinaigrette:
salt
freshly ground black pepper
½ teaspoon Dijon mustard
pinch of sugar
1 tablespoon white wine vinegar
3 tablespoons walnut oil, or 2 tablespoons walnut oil and 1 tablespoon sunflower oil if you like a less assertive flavour

Preparation time: about 10 minutes

ABOVE LEFT: Pease soup
BELOW LEFT: Walnut, beetroot and chicory salad

While poets might be wanly lyrical when their thoughts turn to autumn, I am as likely to think about a new jumper, or perhaps 'wet' walnuts. One of the virtues of food is that each season, however it gets you emotionally, brings compensations. As winter approaches, game, white truffles, mussels, Muscat grapes and, indeed, 'wet', or 'green', walnuts, the fresh new season nuts from France, can take your mind off the clocks going back.

These nuts are a fleeting pleasure and should not be missed. They are new enough to be crushed in your hand and pliable enough to allow the slightly bitter skin on the nut to be rubbed off easily. If it proves obstinate and you are feeling perfectionist, pour boiling water on to the shelled nuts, leave for 2 minutes and drain: the skins will rub off in a trice. I am so keen on new season walnuts that I like to eat them with just the accompaniment of good brown bread, unsalted butter, some Maldon salt and quite a few glasses of wine.

When fresh walnuts are to hand, it is also the moment to lash out on a bottle of walnut oil to make this wonderful first course salad. Make several, in fact, because once opened walnut oil does not keep well and it is expensive.

1. Trim the chicory and slice it diagonally into 1 cm (½ in) pieces.
2. Wash the lamb's lettuce or frisée if you have managed to get hold of either of them. Mix the salad leaves.
3. Make a vinaigrette by dissolving the salt, pepper, mustard, and sugar in the vinegar and whisking in the oil.
4. Dice the beetroot, add to the greens and toss with the vinaigrette.
5. Scatter the salad with the shelled and broken walnuts. Thin slices of a crisp eating apple is a thought as a variation in ingredients.

KIPPER FILLET SALAD

SERVES 4–6
8 kipper fillets
1 large onion, peeled and sliced into thin rings
2 tablespoons lemon juice
olive oil, for dressing
freshly ground black pepper

Preparation time: 5 minutes, plus marinading

In the late sixties this dish became a cliché of the bistros that were opening up all over the place and at dinner parties, which was the way some of us felt constrained to enjoy ourselves. So commonplace was it – not cooking the kippers seemed sort of *daring* at the time – that I stopped making it despite the fact my husband used to say plaintively that he liked it. However, it is good and quick to do and, though no one would be fooled by the idea that raw kippers served with brown bread and butter are somehow like smoked salmon, they have virtue, especially if you use a good olive oil to dress them.

When you buy the packets of kipper fillets moan loudly to whoever will listen about the unnecessary addition of the artificial colour, Brown FK. As Jane Grigson says, it would be interesting to meet that mythical idiot housewife who will only buy spherical watery tomatoes, refusing to consider any other type, and is so nervous about kippers that she needs to be lulled into buying them by their dark brown dye.

1. Rip the silvery skin off the kipper fillets and then slice the fillets on the diagonal into strips about 5 mm (¼ inch) wide.
2. Place them in a shallow dish and scatter half the onion rings on top. Pour on lemon juice. You may need more to ensure that all the pieces will be affected by the juice.
3. Leave it in the fridge for a few hours, turning occasionally.
4. Drain off the juice. Pour on olive oil, enough to dress the kipper pieces generously. Scatter on the remaining onion rings – you then have two textures of onion – and grind on black pepper enthusiastically.
5. Serve as a first course with brown bread and butter.

CARROT PÂTÉ

50 g (2 oz) skinned almonds
225 g (8 oz) carrots
100 g (4 oz) ricotta cheese
1½ teaspoons cumin seeds
4 rashers of streaky bacon
vegetable oil, as required
salt
freshly ground black pepper
pitta bread, to serve

Preparation time: about 15 minutes
Cooking time: 5–10 minutes

One vegetable my vegetable-loathing son, Ben, will countenance is raw carrots. I think he actually quite likes them, though he would sooner die than admit this. However, he would be particularly suspicious of this recipe. Don't you be, because despite the rather odd amalgam of ingredients it turns out to make a delicious first course. Serve with hot pitta bread.

1. Using a food processor fitted with a steel blade, chop the almonds quite roughly. Remove them.
2. Peel the carrots and chop them finely in the machine (If necessary, you can grate the carrots rather than chop them.)
3. Put the ricotta cheese in a bowl, break it up with a fork and add the carrots and almonds. Mix well.
4. In a heavy-bottomed frying pan, toast 1 teaspoon of the cumin seeds (without any oil) until you can smell their spiciness. Add to the carrot mixture.
5. Cut up the bacon finely and fry until crisp. Drain and add to the mixture.
6. Mix well again with enough oil to moisten but not swamp; season and press into individual small pots or one large bowl. Sprinkle the remaining cumin seeds on top. Serve with hot pitta bread.

ABOVE RIGHT: Kipper fillet salad
BELOW RIGHT: Carrot pâté

GRILLED GOAT'S CHEESE WITH SALAD

PER PERSON
1 slice good white or brown bread
1 Chavignol goat's cheese (often sold from a jar of olive oil) or other goat's cheese
black pepper
interesting salad leaves, eg frisée (curly endive), lamb's lettuce (mâche), radicchio, watercress
vinaigrette made with good olive oil or walnut oil

Preparation time: about 5–10 minutes
Cooking time: about 10 minutes

This happens to be a fashionable first course in French restaurants, but it also can make a quick and stylish supper at home. If you are embarking on a more formal meal, then you could serve your cheese and salad course combined in this manner. It will look as though you have gone to a lot of trouble, but what you have also accomplished is being economical in the cheese buying; there will not be a lot of little leftover wedges mocking you from the fridge or larder.

1. Toast the bread. Put it in an ovenproof dish.
2. Place the cheese on top. Grind on some black pepper. Grill for a few minutes until the cheese is lightly browned and bubbling.
3. Serve with the dressed salad on the plate.

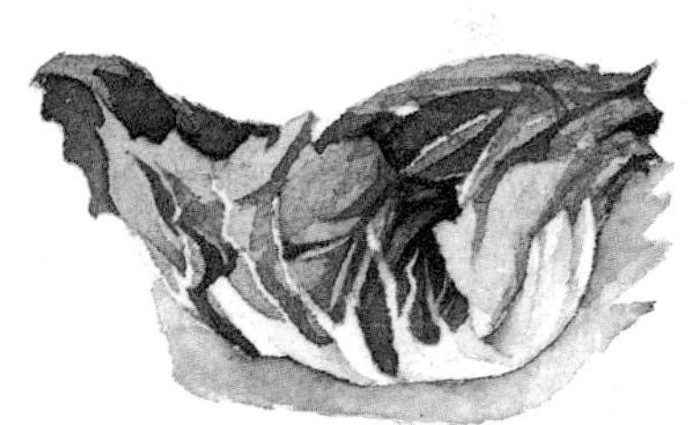

STUFFED MUSHROOMS

SERVES 4–6
6 streaky bacon rashers, chopped
12 large flat mushrooms
4 hard-boiled eggs, shelled
2 thick slices white bread
little single cream or top of the milk
1 fat clove garlic, peeled and chopped
1 tablespoon chopped parsley
salt
freshly ground black pepper
50 g (2 oz) Gruyère or Lancashire cheese, grated

Preparation time: about 25 minutes
Cooking time: about 30 minutes
Oven: 200°C, 400°F, Gas Mark 6
Microwave time: about 15 minutes

ABOVE LEFT: Grilled goat's cheese with salad
BELOW LEFT: Stuffed mushrooms

Large flat mushrooms, the brown shaggy kind, sometimes as large as 10 cm (4 inches) across, are often a bargain since many people prefer the hygienic look of button mushrooms. Sometimes you can buy a whole trug, for a knockdown price, so it is worth looking for bargains. Field mushrooms have more flavour than cultivated mushrooms (they are a completely different species), but they are also more difficult to find. For stuffing mushrooms, buy the caps as flat and wide as possible.

1. Fry the chopped bacon gently until the fat runs and the bacon is cooked.
2. Pull off the mushroom stalks, and chop and sauté them with the bacon.
3. With a fork break up the hard-boiled eggs to a crumb-like consistency.
4. Whizz the bread in a food processor or blender to make crumbs. Moisten them with cream or milk.
5. Mix the stalks, bacon, eggs, crumbs, garlic and parsley. Season well.
6. Divide between the mushroom caps, patting the stuffing into a mound. Sprinkle with cheese and bake for about 20 minutes.

MICROWAVE
If short of time, this dish can be cooked in the microwave: Cook the bacon on Full (100%) power for 3½–4 minutes, stirring once, until the fat runs. Chop the mushroom stalks and add to the bacon. Cover and cook on Full (100%) power for 1 minute. Stuff the mushrooms as described in steps 3–6, then cook in two separate batches on a large plate or microwave tray on Full (100%) for 4–6 minutes.

CELERIAC REMOULADE WITH ANCHOVY TOASTS

1 large celeriac, trimmed and peeled

Mayonnaise:
about 300 ml (½ pint) vegetable oil
2 egg yolks, well beaten
1 dessertspoon Dijon mustard
salt
freshly ground black pepper
squeeze of lemon juice

Anchovy toasts:
1 × 50 g (2 oz) can anchovies, drained of oil
50 g (2 oz) butter
3 slices bread

Preparation time: about 30 minutes
Cooking time: about 10 minutes

I once had Alan Coren to dinner and, let me tell you, he is a picky eater. Much to my surprise, he loved the celeriac remoulade and ate large quantities of it in favour, as I remember, of a particularly delicious home-made brawn. Celeriac is that knobbly beige root, tinging to green at the base, with some fronds en brosse at the top. You can cook it; I like it mashed in equal quantities with potato. But best of all I like it raw, grated and mixed with a mustardy mayonnaise for this remoulade. Some recipe books tell you to blanch it but I think it is unnecessary and also, however careful you are, the process ends by thinning the mayonnaise. Accompanied by the spirited flavour of anchovy toasts, this makes a fine, substantial first course.

1. Make the mayonnaise by dribbling the oil on to the well beaten egg yolks until the emulsion thickens. Flavour it strongly with mustard, salt and pepper and the lemon juice.
2. Grate the celeriac and mix with the mayonnaise immediately, giving it no time to discolour. Taste and adjust the seasoning, if necessary.
3. To make the anchovy toasts, mash 3–4 anchovies into the butter. Toast slices of bread on one side. Spread the untoasted side with the anchovy butter and put under the grill, anchovy butter side up, until the butter is melted and the bread crisp.
4. Cut into fingers and serve with the celeriac.

CONFUCIUS SALAD

4 wind-dried sausages (obtainable in Chinese supermarkets)
mixture of green salad leaves incorporating, if possible, young spinach
3 tablespoons vegetable oil (preferably sunflower), and more for frying
1 tablespoon red wine vinegar
salt
freshly ground black pepper
dry mustard powder
3 slices sesame-seed covered bread or 3 slices white bread and 1 dessertspoon sesame seeds

Preparation time: about 20–25 minutes
Cooking time: about 10 minutes

I feel that this particular example of combining cultures – East and West – is my own. It is part that restaurant cliché, a first course of a salad with bacon and croûtons; part a succumbing to that potent aniseedy flavour the Chinese like so much in their wind-dried sausages; part homage to Confucius. Thus . . .

1. With a small sharp knife, trim the ends of the sausages and then slice them thinly on the diagonal.
2. Wash and dry the salad leaves and heap them into a bowl.
3. Prepare a salad dressing with the oil, vinegar, a pinch of salt, pepper and dry mustard.
4. Assemble a steamer if you have one, or, failing that, find a metal sieve that fits snugly into the top of a saucepan. Boil water in the bottom saucepan and put in the sausage slices to stem.
5. Cut the bread into small cubes and fry in the oil until crisp and golden. If using white bread, fry the sesame seeds in the oil. Drain the croûtons on kitchen paper.
6. Add the bread to the salad, then the sausage after it has been steamed for 3–5 minutes. Pour on the dressing, toss the salad and serve immediately.
7. I once suggested this salad as a dinner party first course to a man friend of mine and I hear he now serves little else. Wind-dried sausages have a particular elusive, addictive flavour and also the advantage of keeping well in the refrigerator; thus they can be always on hand to steam and serve with boiled rice for a quick meal.

ABOVE RIGHT: Celeriac remoulade with anchovy toasts
BELOW RIGHT: Confucius salad

EGGS AND CHEESE

Eggs and cheese have long been recognized as among the most nourishing of convenience foods. These dishes are quick and easy, and in Fay Maschler's expert hands they are never boring, as demonstrated by Eggs Lucullus, baked in creamy nests of lettuce and mushrooms, or the Californian-inspired Designer Pizza with its expensive fashionable ingredients.

Designer pizza

CHEESE AND SPINACH SOUFFLÉ WITH ANCHOVY SAUCE

450 g (1 lb) fresh spinach
50 g (2 oz) butter
3 tablespoons plain flour
300 ml (½ pint) milk
100 g (4 oz) full fat soft cheese
25 g (1 oz) Parmesan cheese, grated, (optional)
salt
freshly ground black pepper
4 eggs, separated

Anchovy Sauce:
1 × 50 g (2 oz) can anchovies, drained of oil or brine
25 g (1 oz) butter
150 ml (¼ pint) double cream

Preparation time: about 15–20 minutes
Cooking time: 40–45 minutes
Oven: 190°C, 375°F, Gas Mark 5

This soufflé is inspired by one of the more famous first courses served by Richard Shepherd at Langan's Brasserie. However, this is not his recipe.

Most of the work can be done well before the meal. When you serve the dish, stab the soufflé dramatically with a spoon and pour the sauce into the middle.

Friends will applaud your insouciance in the face of a culinary marvel and any dryness or monotony in the soufflé will be obviated by the tingling, hot, creamy anchovy.

1. Wash the spinach leaves, trim off any hard stalks and cook the leaves in the water that clings to them until it is tender. Drain in a colander and, when it is cool enough, squeeze it with your hands to get it as dry as possible. Chop it finely.
2. Melt the butter, and stir in the flour to make a roux. Slowly add the milk until you have a thick, smooth sauce and then beat in the soft cheese, bit by bit. Add the Parmesan if you are using it. Stir in the spinach and season quite vigorously. Let cool a little and beat in the egg yolks one by one. All this can be done ahead of time.
3. When you are ready to cook, whip the egg whites until stiff. Fold about a quarter of them into the soufflé mixture to lighten it, then fold in the rest with an even gentler hand.
4. Pour into a buttered soufflé dish and bake in the preheated oven for 25–30 minutes.
5. To make the sauce, soak 5–6 anchovy fillets in warm water briefly, then pat them dry. Melt the butter, add the fillets, stir around until they break up and then pour in the cream. Bring to the boil, give a quick bubble and serve.

BAKED EGGS

15 g (½ oz) butter for each egg
1–2 eggs for each person
salt
freshly ground black pepper
1 tablespoon cream for each egg
1 tablespoon freshly chopped parsley

Possible additions:
a few mushrooms, chopped and sautéed in butter with some cream stirred in and a grating of nutmeg to flavour
a large tomato, skinned, chopped and seeded, tossed in a little butter
some thinly cut ham fried in a little butter

Preparation time: about 10 minutes
Cooking time: about 10 minutes
Oven: 180°C, 350°F, Gas Mark 4

The important point about baked eggs is to cook them so that the white sets but the yolk remains soft. To this end it is sensible to put together a bain-marie – that is, a pan containing hot water in which the cocottes or ramekins can sit. The recipe below is the master recipe for oeufs en cocotte à la crème, with some suggestions for what you might tuck beneath the eggs.

1. If you are using the top of the stove method, find a large pan to which you have a lid or cover and put in enough water to come about halfway up the sides of the ramekins. Place the cocottes in the water in the pan, add the butter and set on a low heat until the butter is melted. Put in whatever extras you want, then slip an egg into each cocotte. Season lightly and cover the pan.
2. After a few minutes, when the eggs have begun to set, pour on a tablespoon of cream, cover again and cook a few minutes more.
3. For cooking in the oven, set the ramekins in a baking tin with hot water and cook gently, uncovered, for about 10 minutes, adding the cream halfway through. When you take the ramekins from the pan, they will continue to cook the egg a little. Garnish with freshly chopped parsley.

ABOVE RIGHT: Cheese and spinach soufflé with anchovy sauce
BELOW RIGHT: Baked eggs

DAL WITH CRACKLING EGGS

275-350 g (10–12 oz) red lentils
2 onions
salt
freshly ground black pepper
1 tablespoon vegetable oil
3–4 hard-boiled eggs
a large pinch of garam masala or curry powder
a small pinch of black mustard seeds (optional)
plain unsweetened yogurt, to serve
sprigs of fresh coriander, to garnish

Preparation time: about 15 minutes
Cooking time: about 35 minutes

I always have some lentils, including the small orange variety sometimes called Egyptian lentils, that cook quickly to a sludge. In Indian shops they are called masoor dal. Frying hard-boiled egg slices in spices resulted in eggs with a texture quite unlike eggs in any other form. Onions fried to a crisp complete this rather delicious meal.

1. Swill the lentils about in a bowl of water to remove chaff and foreign bodies. Cover the drained lentils with fresh water so that there is about 1 cm (½ inch) of water over the lentils in a saucepan. Bring to the boil.
2. Peel and slice the onions, cutting from root to tip to make crescents.
3. Watch the dal. It will cook to a mush in about 20 minutes but might need some additional water. Season the dal with salt and pepper.
4. Fry the onions in a little vegetable oil until brown and crisp. Set aside and keep warm. Clean the pan with kitchen paper.
5. Slice the hard-boiled eggs thickly. Heat a little more oil in the pan, add a good pinch of garam masala or curry powder and the mustard seeds, if you are using them. Fry until the seeds pop, add the egg slices and cook, turning them once or twice until a bubbly crust forms.
6. Serve the dal with the eggs and onion and a bowl of yogurt alongside. Garnish with fresh coriander.

DESIGNER PIZZA

450 g (1 lb) pizza dough mix
1 × 14 oz (400 g) can peeled tomatoes or 2 cartons sieved fresh tomatoes
1 dessertspoon olive oil
a splash of red wine
salt
freshly ground black pepper
a pinch of sugar
3 sun-dried tomatoes, sliced or 1 dessertspoon tomato paste
75 g (3 oz) prosciutto or other raw ham
175 g (6 oz) goat's cheese, crumbled
1 tablespoon chopped fresh basil or 1 teaspoon dried basil
2 garlic cloves, peeled and finely slivered

Preparation time: 10 minutes, plus making pizza dough
Cooking time: 25–35 minutes, plus cooling
Oven: 230°C, 450°F, Gas Mark 8

ABOVE LEFT: Dal with crackling eggs
BELOW LEFT: Designer pizza

The designer pizza is everywhere in America. Gone are the pepperoni sausage, mushrooms, chopped green peppers and Mozzarella cheese, to be replaced by tomato coulis, prosciutto, roasted red peppers, shiitake mushrooms, chèvre and virgin olive oil. Basil has ousted oregano. Expensive and delectable toppings are the key to designer pizza, plus a thin, crisp bread dough base. Dedicated slimmers use tortillas. A fast food has been transformed into a fine food and it will happen here in London's restaurants once customers are prepared to pay for it.

The recipe below is only a guideline. Once you have grasped the concept, you can invent your own creations, incorporating all the fashionable ingredients such as radicchio, sun-dried tomatoes, yellow pepper purée, Peking Duck, enoki mushrooms, confit of garlic, ricotta, grilled aubergine, tapénade (olive purée), and so forth. Go carefully, though; balance is the essence. You can, and probably should, make your own pizza dough, and a nice touch is to incorporate an ingredient like chopped spring onions into it. But you can do this even with a pizza dough mix and that is what I am advising here.

1. Prepare the pizza dough according to the packet instructions. Roll out thinly and line the pizza pan(s) or cake tins.
2. Either drain the canned tomatoes and put them into a saucepan or empty the contents of the carton of sieved tomatoes into one. Add the olive oil, a splash of red wine, salt, pepper and a pinch of sugar. Reduce over heat until you have a spreadable purée. Towards the end add the sun-dried tomatoes or, failing them, tomato paste. Taste for seasoning. Let cool.
3. Cover the dough with the tomato mixture. Arrange the prosciutto slices prettily and scatter on the goat's cheese. Dot with the basil and garlic.
4. Bake for 15-20 minutes or until the crust is crisp and gold.

CHEESE FONDUE

SERVES 6–8
1 garlic clove, peeled
350 ml (12 fl oz) dry white wine
1 teaspoon lemon juice
350 g (12 oz) Gruyère cheese, coarsely grated
225 g (8 oz) Emmenthal cheese, grated
1 heaped teaspoon cornflour
50 ml (2 fl oz) Kirsch or clear fruit brandy or more white wine
freshly ground black pepper
a little grated nutmeg
2 baguettes, sliced
pinch of bicarbonate soda

Preparation time: about 10 minutes
Cooking time: 15–20 minutes

A friend who used to do a job as a chalet party girl in ski resorts tells me that the only time the guests did not fall asleep over their evening meal was when she served cheese fondue. Then people stayed lively and chatty and confessed to having a whale of a time.

If you do not have a fondue set, improvise with a flameproof casserole, a spirit lamp or electric ring and some forks.

1. Rub the fondue dish with the garlic and pour in the white wine. Heat the wine slowly and add the lemon juice.
2. Sprinkle in the cheeses, and slowly bring the mixture to the boil, stirring all the while.
3. Dissolve the cornflour in a small glass of Kirsch, brandy or white wine and when the cheese mixture has melted and become creamy, stir it in. The cornflour helps thicken the fondue and ensures a silky texture.
4. Season with pepper and nutmeg and pass round pieces of crusty bread for dipping. If the mixture should separate and the cheese take on the look of chewing gum, a pinch of bicarbonate of soda usually works like magic.
5. When the cheese has been reduced to a crust on the bottom, splash in another bit of Kirsch, set it alight and, when the flames have died down, divide 'the croûton' among the guests.

OEUFS FLORENTINE

SERVES 2–4
750 g–1 kg (1½–2 lb) fresh spinach or 1 × 450 g (1 lb) packet frozen spinach
40 g (1½ oz) butter or vegetable oil
salt
freshly ground black pepper
a scraping of nutmeg
4 eggs
1 teaspoon vinegar

Sauce:
25 g (1 oz) butter
1 tablespoon flour
300 ml (½ pint) skimmed milk, or half stock and half single cream
50–75 g (2–3 oz) grated Gruyère cheese, plus 25 g (1 oz) freshly grated Parmesan, or 75–100 g (3–4 oz) grated Cheddar
salt
freshly ground black pepper

Preparation time: 5–10 minutes
Cooking time: 30 minutes
Oven: 200°C, 400°F, Gas Mark 6

This is not a breakthrough recipe, just one of those tried and true ideas that sometimes one forgets about in the flurry of being cute and original. It is usually possible to make the dish from ingredients you have to hand, particularly if you choose to use frozen spinach, but fresh spinach is preferable. Fresh spinach can be cooked in the water that clings to its leaves after washing, then drained and left for a while before the final sautéeing in butter or oil.

1. Cook fresh spinach in a large pan until wilted – a matter of minutes. Drain, let cool and squeeze out excess water with your hands. Follow packet instructions for frozen spinach. Chop the fresh spinach or frozen leaf spinach finely.
2. Make the sauce by melting the butter, stirring in the flour and cooking over a gentle heat for a minute or two. Add milk or stock and cream, stirring conscientiously until you have a smooth sauce. Add the grated Gruyère – or 50–75 g (2–3 oz) of the Cheddar – a pinch of salt and pepper and stir until the cheese is melted. Keep the sauce warm.
3. Sauté the spinach in the butter or oil and season with salt, pepper and nutmeg. Spread in a warm ovenproof dish and keep warm.
4. Poach the eggs in simmering water into which you have put the teaspoon of vinegar.
5. Drain the eggs, lay them on the spinach and cover with the cream sauce. Sprinkle on the Parmesan or remaining Cheddar cheese, and give them a few minutes in a hot oven to bring everything to a satisfactory heat.

ABOVE RIGHT: Cheese fondue
BELOW RIGHT: Oeufs Florentine

TUMBET

2 green or red sweet peppers
3 large onions
4 potatoes, peeled
2 courgettes
3 tablespoons olive oil
4 eggs, beaten and seasoned
15 g (½ oz) butter
75 g (3 oz) breadcrumbs

Tomato sauce:
450 g (1 lb) tomatoes, peeled or 1 × 400 g (14 oz) can peeled tomatoes
a little olive oil
1 teaspoon sugar
oregano or fresh basil

Preparation time: about 25 minutes
Cooking time: about 45 minutes
Oven: 180°C, 350°F, Gas Mark 4
Microwave time: 37 minutes

Tumbet is good supper food and is excellent for those late for a meal.

The breadcrumbs are an important element. If you have a food processor, fresh breadcrumbs can be made quickly. Otherwise, you will have to resort to a grater, or drying the bread in the oven and crumbling it with your fingers.

1. To make the tomato sauce, cook the tomatoes in the oil with some salt, pepper, the sugar and herb until pulpy.
2. Meanwhile, core and seed the peppers and cut them into strips. Peel the onions and cut into rings. Cube the potatoes. Wash and slice the courgettes.
3. Fry these ingredients in the olive oil until the potatoes are almost cooked.
4. Grease an earthenware casserole with the butter. Coat with breadcrumbs. Put in a layer of vegetables. Pour over a little beaten egg and some tomato sauce. Repeat this process, finishing with egg.
5. Sprinkle the dish with more breadcrumbs and bake in the preheated oven for 30 minutes until crusty and golden.

MICROWAVE
Place the tomatoes, oil, seasoning and herbs in a bowl. Cook on Full (100%) power for 6 minutes, stirring once. Follow step 2. Place onions, peppers and oil in a bowl. Cover and cook on Full (100%) power for 8 minutes. Stir once. Add the potatoes, mixing well. Cover and cook on Full (100%) power for 10 minutes. Stir once. Add the courgettes, mixing well. Cover and cook on Full (100%) power for 3 minutes, stirring once. Preheat combination oven to 200°C. Follow step 4. Sprinkle the dish with more breadcrumbs. Combination bake at 200°C on Medium (50%) power for 10 minutes. Allow to stand for 5 minutes.

EGGS LUCULLUS

SERVES 2–4
100 g (4 oz) mushrooms
1 round lettuce
25 g (1 oz) butter
1 small garlic clove, peeled and slivered
salt
freshly ground black pepper
1 tablespoon chopped fresh parsley
4 eggs
50 ml (2 fl oz) double cream
25 g (1 oz) Gruyère, Cheddar or Caerphilly cheese, grated

Preparation time: about 20 minutes
Cooking time: about 20–25 minutes
Oven: 180°C, 350°F, Gas Mark 4

ABOVE LEFT: Tumbet
BELOW LEFT: Eggs Lucullus

The usual response to a lettuce is to make a green salad, but, let me tell you, it can also be very nice when cooked. When I cook peas, I always stir in strips of lettuce as they contribute a nice silky texture, and lettuce soup is a delicate first course. Pouring a hot dressing, such as bacon fat mixed with a little wine vinegar, on to lettuce wilts it in an interesting way. In this recipe you get three varieties of softness: the eggs, the mushrooms and the lettuce. If you can find oyster mushrooms or shiitake mushrooms, both now sold in supermarkets as well as Chinese stores, they will make this dish particularly good.

1. Wipe the mushrooms with a damp cloth if they need it and slice them fairly thinly. Wash the lettuce, if necessary, and cut it into strips.
2. Melt the butter, add the mushrooms and garlic and cook gently until they soften. Stir in the lettuce and cook only a few minutes until that, too, is listless.
3. Pour off all the liquid, season the lettuce and mushrooms well and stir in to the parsley.
4. Spread the mixture in an ovenproof dish that will hold four eggs. Using the back of a spoon, make four indentations in the lettuce mixture and break an egg into each of them. Spoon the cream on top and then sprinkle on the cheese.
5. Bake for 12–15 minutes, until the egg white is set but the yolks are still soft and the cheese melted.

CROÛTONS OMELETTE

SERVES 2
4 eggs
2 teaspoons cold water
salt
freshly ground black pepper
a few springs of parsley, chopped
1 small bundle chives, finely chopped
1 fat garlic clove, peeled and chopped
2 slices brown bread, cut into small cubes
vegetable oil
25 g (1 oz) Parmesan cheese, grated
1 bunch spring onions, trimmed and finely chopped
40 g (1½ oz) butter

Preparation time: about 10 minutes
Cooking time: 20–40 minutes

Determined not to make an omelette *nature,* for a friend of mine, I used what was around and composed a filling of brown bread croûtons flavoured by garlic and quickly fried chopped spring onions. It was a successful combination. The crunch of croûtons provided edgy relief from the softness of egg and, because it was wholemeal bread, it also lent a nutty flavour. Had I had some Parmesan cheese, I would have tossed the croûtons in that, so I have added it to the instructions below.

1. I like to cook omelettes one at a time. If you are of this persuasion, break 2 eggs into a bowl, and add 1 teaspoon cold water. Season with salt and pepper and add half the herbs. Beat lightly.
2. Heat some vegetable oil in a small frying pan with the garlic and fry the bread, turning until you have croûtons crisp on all sides. Roll them in Parmesan cheese. Keep warm.
3. In the same oil quickly fry the spring onions. Drain on kitchen paper and keep warm.
4. Heat half the butter in an omelette pan. When it is foaming, add the beaten eggs. Push them and lift them, as you do with an omelette and, when set on the bottom and tacky on the surface, scatter on half the croûtons and onions.
5. Fold over, tip out and serve with a little butter rubbed on top of the omelette to give it gloss.
6. Repeat the procedure with the other two eggs. Alternatively, make one large omelette.

INDIAN SCRAMBLED EGGS

SERVES 3
3 tablespoons vegetable oil, or ghee or butter
1 onion, peeled and finely sliced
1 cm (½ inch) cube fresh ginger, grated
1 small hot green chilli, seeded and cut into threads
¼ teaspoon ground turmeric
½ teaspoon ground cumin
1 tomato, peeled, seeded and chopped
6 eggs
salt
freshly ground black pepper
1 tablespoon chopped coriander leaves

To serve:
toast or fried bread

Preparation time: 5–10 minutes
Cooking time: 15–20 minutes

The combination of chilli and eggs is particularly good and, even if you do not have all the spices mentioned below, just a little fried fresh green chilli stirred into eggs makes a dish substantially different to the usual breakfast assembly. Eggs prepared this way are served all over India, but the influence is from the Parsees, a Zoroastrian community that fled Persia in the eighth century because of Moslem persecution. Their cuisine, which benefits from few strictures, is especially inventive where egg dishes are concerned.

1. Heat the oil or fat in a sauté pan and fry the onion until golden. Add the ginger, chilli, turmeric and cumin and stir around. Add the tomato and cook gently for about 3 minutes.
2. Beat the eggs lightly and season them. Add to the spicy onion mixture and stir over a low heat as you do for scrambled eggs.
3. Just before they are ready, stir in the fresh coriander. Serve either with toast or with fried bread.

ABOVE RIGHT: Croûtons omelette
BELOW RIGHT: Indian scrambled eggs

PASTA AND RICE

The beauty of pasta or rice is that it can take pretty much anything which you care to add to it. Even macaroni cheese is transformed in Fay Maschler's rich version. Try delicious Risotto or Risi e Bisi, and use the proper Italian rice for a melting, creamy texture.

Pasta with smoked trout

PASTA WITH FRESH TOMATOES AND BASIL

450 g (1 lb) pasta of choice
salt
a dribble of olive oil

Sauce:
4 tomatoes or 2 beefsteak tomatoes, skinned and chopped
4 spring onions, cleaned and finely chopped
1 tablespoon finely chopped parsley
10–12 fresh basil leaves, roughly chopped
3 tablespoons good olive oil
1 tablespoon red wine vinegar
freshly ground black pepper

Preparation time: about 10 minutes
Cooking time: 5–10 minutes

When fresh basil with its smell of summer is around, try this sauce, which is one of my favourites with fresh pasta. The point is its freshness and coolness, in contrast to the hot pasta.

1. Cook the pasta in plenty of boiling, salted water to which you have added a dribble of olive oil. Drain well and heap into a warm bowl.
2. To make the sauce, mix together all the ingredients and, at the moment of serving, pour the cold sauce on to the hot drained pasta.

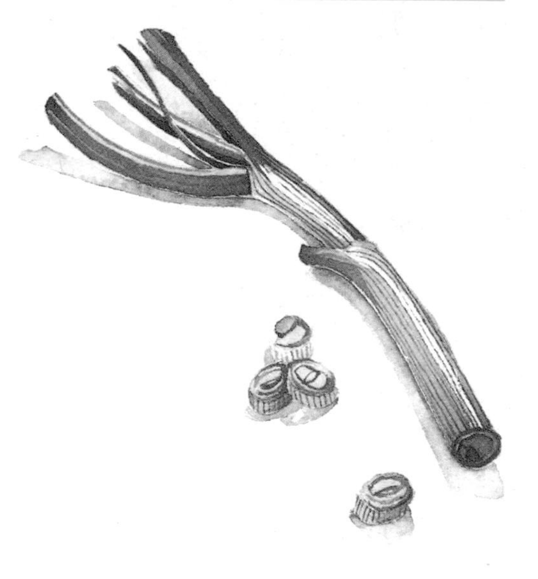

NICE MACARONI CHEESE

225–275 g (8–10 oz) macaroni (whole wheat, if you wish)
salt
1 tablespoon oil
6 sweet-cured, streaky bacon rashers
40 g (1½ oz) butter, plus extra to grease dish
1 onion, peeled and finely chopped
2 level tablespoons flour
450 ml (¾ pint) milk
splash of white wine
175 g (6 oz) farmhouse Cheddar cheese, grated
50 g (2 oz) Parmesan cheese, freshly grated
a pinch of English mustard powder
freshly ground black pepper
1 large beefsteak tomato, sliced
1 tablespoon fresh breadcrumbs

Preparation time: about 10 minutes
Cooking time: 40-45 minutes
Oven: 200°C, 400°F, Gas Mark 6

I call this nice macaroni cheese because I have had, and no doubt you have had, the horrid variety; mean, pallid and gluey. However, as with many dishes associated with childhood or institutions, there is a punitive way of making it and an enticing way of making it. The key to the latter, as indeed the key to any good recipe, is the quality of the basic ingredients. If you use freshly grated Parmesan cheese, farmhouse Cheddar, sweet-cured streaky bacon, a splash of white wine in the sauce and unsalted butter in the roux, you will end up with perhaps not a sophisticated or startling dish but a jolly nice supper.

1. Boil the macaroni in masses of salted water, into which you have put a spoonful of oil until the pasta is tender – about 10–15 minutes. Drain.
2. Chop the bacon and fry it until fairly crisp. Drain on kitchen paper and then mix into the macaroni.
3. Melt the butter and fry the onion gently until softened but not browned. Stir in the flour and cook for a minute or two. Gradually add the milk, then the wine, stirring until you have a smooth sauce. Add the Cheddar cheese and half the Parmesan. Stir off the heat until the cheese is melted and add a good pinch of mustard. Season with black pepper.
4. Fold the macaroni into the sauce. Turn into a buttered shallow baking dish. Arrange the sliced tomato on top. Scatter on the crumbs which you have mixed with the remaining Parmesan.
5. Heat through in the preheated oven until the top is crisped. Serve with a green salad as an accompaniment.

ABOVE RIGHT: Pasta with fresh tomatoes and basil
BELOW RIGHT: Nice macaroni cheese

TABBOULEH

SERVES 4–6
100 g (4 oz) cracked wheat
1 bunch spring onions, trimmed and finely chopped
2 large tomatoes
75 g (3 oz) fresh parsley, washed and finely chopped
3 tablespoons finely chopped fresh mint (less if dried)
3 tablespoons lemon juice
3 tablespoons olive oil
salt
freshly ground black pepper
lettuce leaves, to serve
lemon slices, to garnish

Preparation time: about 30 minutes

Tabbouleh keeps well for a couple of days; it also makes a delicious first course.

Bulghur or burghul, cracked wheat, is sold in delicatessens, Middle Eastern groceries and health-food shops. It is important to get the substance that looks like tiny grains and not an English variety of cracked wheat that is flaky. If you have no luck finding it, couscous will do almost as well. With its hefty quantity of parsley, tabbouleh is a great source of iron and Vitamin C. Mint adds freshness and lemon sharpness. Once hooked, you can become addicted. The quantities below are a guideline only. Feel free to dabble with the proportions. Middle Eastern recipes have never been very precise. But they are always generous.

1. Pour cold water on to the cracked wheat to cover, and leave to soak and swell for about 1 hour. Drain in a sieve and then squeeze out what water you can with your hands. If the grains still seem waterlogged, spread them on a clean tea-towel, but this is the counsel of perfection.
2. Put the cracked wheat in a bowl, add the spring onions and mix energetically.
3. Plunge the tomatoes into boiling water for a minute. Remove them, peel off the skins and dice the flesh, discarding the pips and juice.
4. Add the chopped tomato, parsley, mint, lemon juice, olive oil, and salt and pepper to taste to the cracked wheat. Mix and taste to see if you wish to emphasize any flavour.
5. Leave for a while so that the flavours develop. Then serve, garnished with slices of lemon. Leaves of iceberg, cos or Webb's lettuce should be offered alongside.

SPAGHETTI ALLA PUTTANESCA

3 tablespoons olive oil and a dribble for cooking the pasta
2–3 garlic cloves, peeled and finely chopped
1 small fresh chilli or 2 dried red chillies
5–6 anchovy fillets, drained of oil or brine and rinsed
100 g (4 oz) large black olives
1 tablespoon capers
1 × 200 g (7 oz) can peeled tomatoes
1 tablespoon tomato paste
450 g (1 lb) spaghetti
salt
freshly ground black pepper
finely chopped dried oregano or parsley

Preparation time: about 10 minutes
Cooking time: about 20 minutes

ABOVE LEFT: Tabbouleh
BELOW LEFT: Spaghetti alla puttanesca

Pasta is the obvious quick, inexpensive meal. Indeed, the teenage son of a friend of mine recently persuaded his father who was looking after him that he deserved a meal in a restaurant on the grounds that he could not be expected to eat pasta again. But for its fattening qualities when put with a sauce and cheese, I would eat pasta at least once a meal and there are probably enough different recipes and varieties that you could do this for a year without repeating a dish. The one below has ingredients easy to assemble from any delicatessen. The name means 'whore's spaghetti', which may refer to its gutsiness or to its sustaining quality. Include the chilli; it makes all the difference.

1. In a sauté pan heat the olive oil and gently cook the garlic and chilli, chopped if you wish or whole if you plan to remove it.
2. Chop the anchovies roughly and add them to the oil. Stir until they break up.
3. Stone and slice the olives, and add them to the sauce with the capers, the tomatoes and tomato paste.
4. Stir and break up the tomatoes and simmer the sauce while you cook the spaghetti in masses of boiling water into which you have put a pinch of salt and a dribble of olive oil. Drain the pasta and heap it into a warm bowl.
5. Taste the sauce and adjust the seasoning. Pour the sauce on to the pasta. Mix in lightly and sprinkle the dish with a little dried oregano or some finely chopped parsley. Green salad, crusty bread and a bottle of robust Italian red wine are the only other requirements.

PASTA WITH ANCHOVIES AND BROCCOLI

450 g (1 lb) broccoli, divided into small florets
4–6 anchovy fillets, drained of oil
2 garlic cloves, peeled and thinly sliced
120 ml (4 fl oz) olive oil
½ fresh chilli, finely chopped, or 2 small red dried chillies
25 g (1 oz) butter
freshly ground black pepper
400 g (14 oz) spaghetti or other pasta

Preparation time: about 5–10 minutes
Cooking time: 15–30 minutes

The pronounced flavour of broccoli contrasts well with that of anchovies. The way they use this combination of flavours as a pasta garnish in Apulia is with garlic and no cheese. You can use spaghetti or any pasta shape – bows might be nice. Make sure you do not overcook the broccoli as it is then apt to turn a depressing grey colour.

1. Bring a large quantity of water to the boil and boil the broccoli florets for a minute or two, keeping them green and crisp. If you like, as I do, to cook the stalks, slice them thinly on the diagonal first. They add yet another texture. Drain the broccoli and keep it warm.
2. Cook the anchovy fillets and the garlic slivers in the oil, stirring and mashing until the anchovies disintegrate. Add the chilli and the butter and stir some more.
3. Turn the broccoli gently in this sauce and grind on some black pepper.
4. Meanwhile cook the pasta; drain and pour on the sauce. Mix carefully and serve, perhaps with an extra dribble of oil.

RISI E BISI

1 onion, peeled and finely chopped
25 g (1 oz) butter, and a little more for serving
50 g (2 oz) raw ham, preferably pancetta or coppa, otherwise streaky bacon
1 kg (2 lb) peas in their pods
salt
900 ml (1½ pints) chicken or veal stock, or a mixture of stock and the water from boiling the pea pods
400 g (14 oz) Italian risotto rice
2 tablespoons chopped fresh parsley, preferably the flat-leafed variety
freshly ground black pepper
50 g (2 oz) Parmesan cheese, freshly grated

Preparation time: about 10 minutes
Cooking time: about 30 minutes

Risi e Bisi (rice and peas) is one of the definitive dishes of Venetian cooking. Traditionally it was offered to the Doges on the feast day of St Mark, the patron saint of the city. When peas are fresh, young and sweet, it is one of the nicest, simplest, dishes imaginable. I remember once interviewing a rather sophisticated art dealer about the food he liked and asking him that predictable question 'What is your favourite dish?' thinking it would be some elaborate confection utilizing rare ingredients. He replied, 'Rice and peas.'

In Venice the dish is made not exactly as a risotto or really a soup, but of a consistency that requires it to be eaten with a spoon. Try to find Arborio rice, which will contribute the correct texture, and, if you have the time and energy, make a stock with the pea pods to moisten the rice. The ham is optional, but does make it more of a meal.

1. Sauté the onion in the butter until softened, then add the chopped ham and stir round for a few minutes. Add shelled peas and a pinch of salt and turn around in the butter.
2. Add 750 ml (1¼ pints) of the stock, cover and simmer for about 10 minutes.
3. Add the washed rice, the parsley and the rest of the stock. Cover again and cook slowly until the rice is tender but retains a bite. Check the seasoning, adding more salt, if necessary, and some freshly ground black pepper.
4. Stir in half the cheese and a dab of butter. Serve, handing the rest of the Parmesan cheese separately.

ABOVE RIGHT: Pasta with anchovies and broccoli
BELOW RIGHT: Risi e bisi

KEDGEREE

SERVES 4–6
375 g (12 oz) smoked haddock
milk to cover fish
225 g (8 oz) basmati rice
2 onions, peeled and thinly sliced
1 tablespoon vegetable oil
50g (2 oz) butter
1 dessertspoon ground turmeric
salt
freshly ground black pepper
3 hard-boiled eggs

Preparation time: 15 minutes
Cooking time: about 25 minutes
Oven: 180°C, 350°F, Gas Mark 4

Kedgeree was what happened when the English met the Indian dish khichri, originally a mixture of lentils, rice and spices and, incidentally, delicious made in that austere way. The additions of smoked haddock, hard-boiled eggs, curry powder or turmeric, cream or whatever else you happen to believe is appropriate or necessary, is just proof of how dishes can evolve fortuitously.

In my household kedgeree has become an institution for breakfast on Christmas Day. It not only gets the day off to a satisfactory start – important given the *tension* of the whole event – but most of the constituent parts can be prepared the night before to be assembled on the morning. This makes it a good dish for any time of year and breakfast, lunch or supper. Finnan haddock, which is the fish smoked on the bone, is infinitely preferable to dyed fillets. And, of course, basmati rice is preferable to boil-in-the-bag, pre-fluffed or that notorious American brand.

1. Put the haddock in an oven dish, add enough milk nearly to cover the fish and cook in a preheated oven for about 20 minutes or until the fish flakes easily.
2. Remove any skin or bones and keep the fish-flavoured milk.
3. Meanwhile, cook the rice, using the method you have found best.
4. Fry the onions in the oil and butter until golden. Add the turmeric and cook it gently for a few minutes.
5. Add the haddock and rice and mix gently until the rice is coloured a rich saffron yellow. Use some of the milk to moisten the mixture and more butter if you like richness.
6. Taste for seasoning and be generous with the pepper. Scatter the dish with chopped hard-boiled eggs.

FRESH PASTA WITH SMOKED TROUT AND FISH EGGS

100 g (4 oz) smoked trout
salt
150 ml (¼ pint) double cream
450 g (1 lb) fresh pasta
4 tablespoons fish eggs, such as caviar, lumpfish roe (known as Danish caviar) or salmon eggs
flat-leaf parsley, to garnish

Preparation time: about 10 minutes
Cooking time: 15–25 minutes

ABOVE LEFT: Kedgeree
BELOW LEFT: Fresh pasta with smoked trout and fish eggs

1. Skin and bone the smoked trout and carefully flake the fish. Set aside.
2. While you set to boil a large pot of salted water for the pasta, reduce the cream slightly in a small pan over medium heat.
3. Cook the pasta until it is *al dente* – if it is fresh this should be only a matter of a minute or two, otherwise consult the packet but test the pasta some time before the suggested cooking time limit.
4. Add the smoked trout to the hot cream and mix carefully with the drained pasta.
5. Divide between four hot plates and crown each heap with small spoonfuls of fish eggs. Garnish with parsley sprigs.

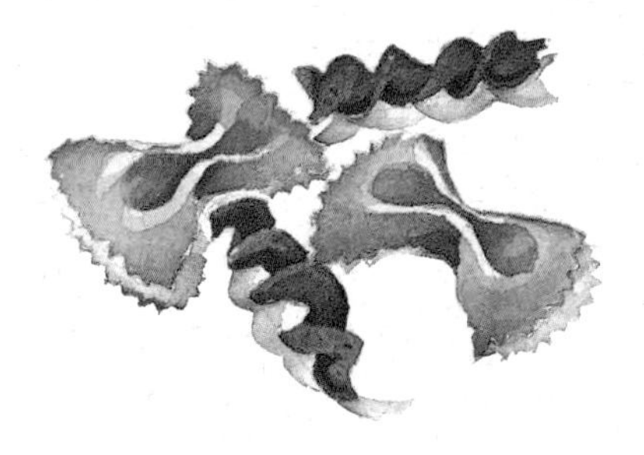

SPAGHETTI CARBONARA

SERVES 3–4
400 g (14 oz) spaghetti
1 teaspoon salt
1 tablespoon olive oil or other vegetable oil
4 eggs
2 tablespoons double cream
2 tablespoons Parmesan cheese, grated
150 g (5 oz) streaky bacon or pancetta ham, thinly sliced
freshly ground black pepper

Preparation time: 5 minutes
Cooking time: 10–15 minutes

My children are never happier than when I answer 'Spaghetti Carbonara' to their question of 'What's for dinner?' I often say this on a day when I have been less than efficient about shopping, for most of the ingredients are usually stock items in the refrigerator. I do not say the words too often though, as you can see Spaghetti Carbonara is not the healthiest of dishes. I have noticed that some people feel fearful about getting it right. If you add some cream to the eggs it obviates the risk of them curdling, but even if they do – if the hot spaghetti 'cooks' them rather too well – the resulting grainy texture is quite pleasant. Try to get pancetta ham from the delicatessen or otherwise use thinly sliced smoked streaky bacon.

1. Boil up a large pot of water for the spaghetti, salt it and add a spoonful of vegetable oil or olive oil to stop the strands sticking together.
2. Beat the eggs with the cream. Stir in the Parmesan.
3. Chop the bacon into small pieces and fry slowly in a heavy frying pan, only adding butter or oil if sufficient fat for cooking is not present in the bacon.
4. Cook the spaghetti and when it is *al dente,* drain it and return it to the pan.
5. Add the bacon and a little of the fat. Mix around. Pour in the egg mixture and toss carefully. This should be done off the heat.
6. Grind on black pepper with the *brio* perfected by Italian waiters and serve on heated plates or in shallow bowls.

RISOTTO WITH DRIED MUSHROOMS

SERVES 4–6
25 g (1 oz) dried mushrooms (porcini are excellent)
1 litre (1¾ pints) light chicken stock
1 onion or 3 shallots, peeled and finely chopped
3 tablespoons vegetable oil
50 g (2 oz) butter
400 g (14 oz) Italian risotto rice
25 g (1 oz) freshly grated Parmesan cheese
salt
freshly ground black pepper

Preparation time: 5 minutes, plus soaking time
Cooking time: about 25 minutes

To make a good risotto you need patience, good stock and Italian risotto rice, often called Arborio rice. This is smaller and stubbier than ordinary long grain or basmati rice and has the quality of turning out slightly sticky, but retaining a chewy kernel, which gives texture to the assembly. I find a carefully made risotto so seductive that I like it in its simplest form using just rice, butter and oil, stock and grated Parmesan cheese, but it has to be admitted that the dried mushrooms and their liquid make it more of a dish. If you want to make a plain version, the instructions still hold. To save time, the mushrooms could be soaked earlier in the day, or overnight.

1. At least half an hour before cooking time, soak the mushrooms in lukewarm water. Drain through a sieve lined with kitchen paper and keep the liquid. Soak them again if you think they need to be softer or cleaner.
2. Bring the stock to simmering point.
3. In a heavy-bottomed pan sauté the onion or shallots in the oil and half the butter until soft.
4. Add the rice and stir until it is absorbed. Continue for about 10 minutes, adding a ladleful of hot stock each time the rice dries out.
5. Add the mushrooms and 150 ml (¼ pint) of the mushroom liquid. As this becomes absorbed, add more mushroom liquid bit by bit until it is finished. If you need more liquid to finish cooking the rice, use stock or hot water.
6. Mix in the rest of the butter and the Parmesan. Taste for saltiness and grind on some black pepper.
7. Turn into a hot serving dish and offer more grated cheese separately.

ABOVE RIGHT: Spaghetti carbonara
BELOW RIGHT: Risotto with dried mushrooms

FISH AND SHELLFISH

Try Clam Chowder for that transatlantic flavour or head east with Sashimi, probably one of the all-time easiest and most delicious of fish dishes. For those who prefer their fish cooked, the Baked Salmon or Herring in Oatmeal are interesting variations of traditional recipes.

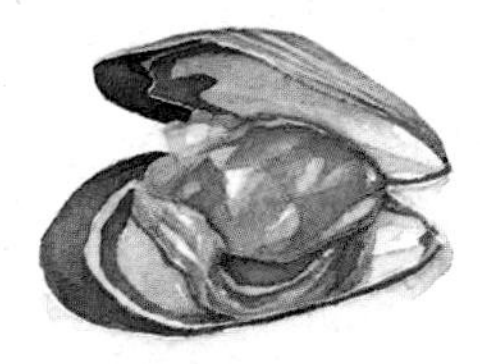

Mussel salad

FISH STEAKS AU POIVRE

4 cod steaks or steaks from other firm-fleshed fish such as halibut or haddock
sea salt
2 heaped tablespoons whole peppercorns
1 tablespoon plain flour
2 tablespoons vegetable oil
50 g (2 oz) butter

Sauce:
300 ml (½ pint) good stock
150 ml (¼ pint) white wine or a squeeze of lemon juice
salt
freshly ground black pepper
a nut of butter or 150 ml (¼ pint) double cream

Preparation time: about 15 minutes
Cooking time: 20–25 minutes

This recipe is quick and mildly impressive and, surprisingly, the flavour of the fish can stand up to the nitty-gritty of black peppercorns. I once very successfully treated a large fresh tuna steak this way, but you seldom find that in the fishmongers and it is expensive when you do. Cod is my recommendation. I think cod is underrated. Try to obtain steaks rather than fillets.

1. Trim the fish, if necessary, to present nice, neat steaks. Sprinkle them with sea salt. Crush the peppercorns coarsely. Mix with the flour. Press this mixture into the fish steaks, covering them as evenly as possible.
2. Heat the oil and butter in a frying pan or sauté pan and cook the steaks carefully, turning once.
3. When the fish is almost cooked – a knife winkled in next to the bone reveals opacity almost right through – pour in the stock down the side of the pan (ie don't douse the fish). When the fish is quite cooked, remove it and keep it warm.
4. To make the sauce, add the wine or lemon juice to the pan and boil it energetically until approximately a cupful of liquid remains. Taste for seasoning and either use the sauce as it is, with a nut of butter whisked in, or add the cream and continue to boil, stirring, until you have a rich, well amalgamated sauce.
5. Check again for seasoning and pour the sauce around, not over, the fish. Plain boiled potatoes or rice are suitable accompaniments.

CLAM CHOWDER

SERVES 3–4
100 g (4 oz) salt pork or a thick slice of gammon or bacon, diced
a little vegetable oil
1 onion, peeled and chopped
3 potatoes, peeled and cut into 1 cm (½ inch) cubes
600 ml (1 pint) milk
1 × 200 g (7 oz) can clams
½ teaspoon dried thyme or fennel seeds
freshly ground black pepper
salt

To serve
a little double cream (optional)
a pinch of cayenne pepper (optional)
chopped fresh parsley
crackers, such as water biscuits

Preparation time: about 10 minutes
Cooking time: about 20–25 minutes

Clam chowder is a Yankee dish often eaten as a meal in itself rather than just as a soup. New Englanders feel very strongly about what should and what should not be included as ingredients and my heart goes out to a certain Maine legislator named Seeder who, in 1939, introduced a bill to make it illegal to add tomatoes to the pot. I think cooked tomatoes add little to any dish, except perhaps tomato sauce, and this soup, traduced by any canned version, is best when it is just a combination of clams, salt pork, potatoes, onions and milk. There is nothing like the selection of clams you find in the States available here, and even though some are appearing in fishmongers, a can of clams in their juice works fine in the recipe below. Find whole clams, not minced ones.

1. Fry the salt pork in a little vegetable oil until it is cooked and the fat is crisped. Remove the pork.
2. Fry the chopped onion until soft, then add the potatoes, milk, juice from the clams, thyme or fennel seeds and pepper. Taste for salt before adding any. Simmer until the potatoes are tender.
3. Stir in the clams and the pork and simmer again until they are heated through.
4. An optional garnish is a swirl of double cream sprinkled with cayenne pepper. In any case try to have some chopped parsley for sprinkling over because the colours of the chowder – the creamy milk, the beige clams and the rosy pork – are enhanced by a flourish of green. Serve in heated bowls with crackers as an accompaniment.

ABOVE RIGHT: Fish steaks au poivre
BELOW RIGHT: Clam chowder

FISH PLAKI

SERVES 4–5
750 g (1½ lb) firm-fleshed white fish
1 lemon, squeezed and sliced afterwards
salt
freshly ground black pepper
3 tablespoons virgin olive oil
2 onions, peeled and finely sliced
2 cloves garlic, peeled and chopped
4 tomatoes, peeled, sliced and seeded
fresh parsley or dill or mint
150 ml (¼ pint) white wine
a pinch of sugar

Preparation time: about 10 minutes
Cooking time: about 1 hour
Oven: 180°C, 350°F, Gas Mark 4

Fish is so much the darling of the *nouvelle cuisine* chefs that there is little these days, in restaurants anyway, between fish in batter as in a chippie and steamed fillets surrounded by some nancy little sauce in high-priced shrines to gastronomy. This Mediterranean method of cooking fish has a welcome robustness. If you are a lover of Greece, as I am, you will probably have encountered fish cooked in this manner with the almost unavoidable, but poignantly summery, mélange of tomatoes, onions, garlic, lemons and olive oil. Any firm-fleshed white fish takes readily to this treatment, but given the price of varieties like halibut and turbot, cod is perhaps most to the point. This is also an amenable dish to varying degrees of temperature; it can be served hot, cold, when the juices turn to a nice jelly, or lukewarm – as in Greece.

1. Sprinkle the fish with some of the lemon juice and season with salt and pepper.
2. In the olive oil, soften the onions and garlic. Add the tomatoes, parsley or dill or mint and white wine. If you are using anaemic-looking tomatoes, put in a pinch of sugar. Cook until the sauce is somewhat reduced and tastes good, using your judgement about more lemon juice, etc.
3. Oil a baking dish. Lay in the fish. Pour on the sauce and arrange slices of the squeezed lemon on top.
4. Cook in a preheated oven for about 45 minutes.

MUSSEL AND POTATO SALAD

750 g (1½ lb) potatoes (a firm waxy variety)
1–1.5 kg (2–3 lb) fresh mussels
3 tablespoons white wine
4 shallots, peeled and chopped
50 g (2 oz) fresh parsley
freshly ground black pepper
about 4 tablespoons vinaigrette

Preparation time: about 20 minutes
Cooking time: about 20 minutes

If you have never tackled fresh live mussels there are a few things worth knowing, one being that you should waste no time in getting to grips with them; they are a reasonable and delicious source of protein. Mussels should be used the day you buy them. They must be thoroughly scrubbed, but with the large English variety with their encrusted shells I do not think it is necessary to scrape off every single barnacle. In this recipe you do not see the shells. Tug off the byssus, the thread by which the mussels cling to stones. Discard any mussels that do not close when tapped – they are dead – and after cooking throw out any that have not opened. Most people know mussels in the form of moules marinière; opened with shallots, white wine, garlic and parsley in the pan. I like the lesser known mouclade, where the resulting liquor is thickened with a roux plus cream, egg yolks and a splash of an anise-based drink like pastis.

1. Scrub the potatoes and boil them in their skins. When they are tender peel them and slice them.
2. Meanwhile, put the mussels in a large pan with the wine, shallots, a couple of springs of parsley and a generous amount of pepper. Set on a high heat, cover and after a few minutes shake the pan. The mussels will open in the boiling liquid and the resulting steam.
3. When all are opened, excluding the duff ones, remove them and strain the mussel liquor through the finest possible sieve over the potatoes. A counsel of perfection would be to line your sieve with muslin or a tea-towel wrung out in hot water.
4. Remove the mussels from the shells.
5. When the potatoes are cool, drain them and mix with the mussels. Dress with vinaigrette and sprinkle with chopped parsley. I like this salad served still lukewarm.

ABOVE LEFT: Fish plaki
BELOW LEFT: Mussel and potato salad

RAIE AU BEURRE NOIR

SERVES 4–6
4 skate wings, about 1 kg (2 lb) in weight
50 g (2 oz) butter
2 tablespoons red wine vinegar
salt
freshly ground black pepper
1 dessertspoon capers
finely chopped parsley

Court Bouillon
2 tablespoons white wine vinegar
1 carrot, sliced
1 onion, peeled and sliced
10 peppercorns
salt
a sprig of parsley

Preparation time: about 10 minutes
Cooking time: 35–40 minutes

What skate has got going for it, apart from its interesting, slightly gelatinous texture, is that, almost uniquely among fish, it is all the better for not being sparklingly fresh. A faint maturity is desirable. The usual test of bright eyes and firm gills is not applicable in any case since skate is sold in 'wings'. Beurre noir, which is butter cooked until it is not really black but a dark, nutty brown, is a useful technique (sauce seems a slight exaggeration) that can be applied to almost anything bland, for example, brains or fried eggs.

1. In a large shallow pan put enough water to cover the skate and add all the flavouring ingredients for the court bouillon. Put in the fish and bring slowly to the boil.
2. After one eruption of bubbles, lower the heat to achieve just below simmering point. Cook the fish for 10–15 minutes until the flesh is opaque down to the main bone. (You can do this in the oven if you feel happier about it.)
3. Drain the fish thoroughly and arrange on a warm serving dish.
4. Melt the butter in a frying pan and, watching like a hawk, cook it until it goes a deep brown. Pour it over the fish.
5. Put into the hot pan 2 tablespoons red wine vinegar, season it with salt and pepper, swirl it around and let it bubble for a few seconds. Pour that over the fish.
6. Scatter over the capers and chopped parsley and serve immediately. Boiled potatoes are the best accompaniment for this dish.

ROASTED FISH WITH ANCHOVY SAUCE

1 whole fish, weighing about 1–1.5 kg (2–3 lb)
fresh herbs (fennel, dill or parsley)
1 bay leaf
1 slice of lemon
salt
freshly ground black pepper
a little olive oil
50 g (2 oz) butter
1 × 50 g (2 oz) can anchovy fillets, drained of oil
300 ml (½ pint) double cream

Preparation time: about 10 minutes
Cooking time: 25–30 minutes
Oven: 220°C, 425°F, Gas Mark 7

A whole fish is easy to cook and turns out much more festive than the googly-eyed creature might suggest. Choose sea bass if you are feeling flush, but the cheaper grey mullet, red bream or haddock actually stand up better to the quite forceful anchovy sauce. It goes well also on boiled vegetables, for example, celeriac or celery or kohlrabi and makes a change from the tuna fish sauce with veal, as in vitello tonnato.

1. Have the fishmonger clean the fish, leaving on the head and tail. Using a small sharp knife, make three diagonal slashes on each side of the fish, cutting practically down to the bone. Tuck herbs and the bay leaf, plus a slice of lemon, into the body cavity. Rub the salt and freshly ground black pepper into the surfaces of the fish, making sure that some topples into the slashes. Trickle olive oil over the fish and place in a roasting pan.
2. Put into the preheated oven. An average-size fish should be cooked in approximately 25–30 minutes. The cuts in the sides will enable you to see if the flesh is opaque to the bone.
3. To make the sauce, melt the butter in a frying pan or sauté pan. Add the anchovies and stir around until they break up and more or less disintegrate. Add the cream, bring to the boil and stir. Add some freshly ground black pepper and taste to see if the sauce could stand the addition of another anchovy. The flavour should be robust.
4. Carefully lift the fish, whose skin should be brown and crisp, on to a serving dish and serve the sauce separately. Serve with boiled potatoes.

ABOVE RIGHT: Raie au beurre noir
BELOW RIGHT: Roasted fish with anchovy sauce

SASHIMI

350 g (12 oz) fillets of fresh fish: choose from salmon, bream, halibut, turbot, trout, sole or whatever else looks good
1 large Japanese radish (daikon) or mooli, or a selection of interesting salad leaves
2 tablespoons wasabi or 6 cm (2½ inch) piece of fresh ginger root
150 ml (¼ pint) light soy sauce (shoyu or tamari)

Preparation time: about 35 minutes

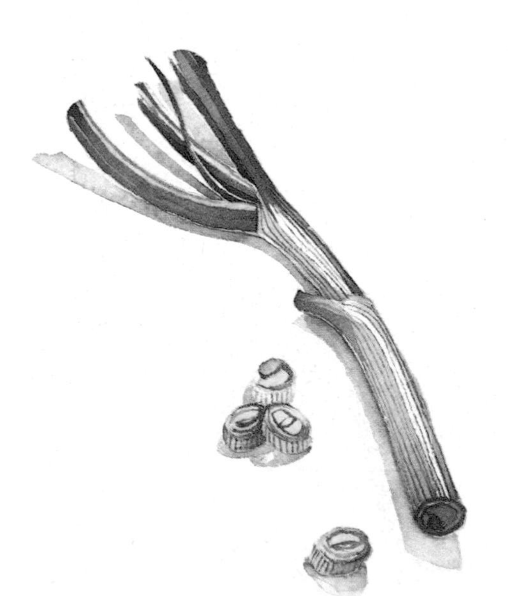

LEFT: Sashimi

If the idea of eating raw fish gives you the willies – but, think, have you eaten oysters? – then this recipe is only of academic interest. But if you have eaten sashimi or sushi in Japanese restaurants or had salads garnished with thinly sliced raw fish, and wished you could recreate the dishes at home for much less money, here is how. What you must have is a fishmonger on whom you can rely to sell you only the freshest fish. Aim to buy two or three varieties of fish to achieve a contrast in colour and texture. The pink of salmon is pretty. Endeavour also to find small tins of powdered Japanese horseradish called wasabi (available in oriental supermarkets) or, failing that, fresh ginger root, for both serve a digestive function as well as being complementary flavours.

1. Trim the fish fillets of any bits of skin or bone and put them in a colander. Pour boiling water over them and then immediately plunge them into cold water. This does not cook the fish, but it does blitz any surface bacteria.
2. Using an exceedingly sharp knife, cut the fish into slices, either thickish or thin according to preference. Aficionados prefer the thick and, be assured, raw fish does not have a fishy flavour.
3. Grate the cleaned radish or salad on to four pretty plates or in four bowls. Arrange the slices of fish as aesthetically as possible on, or beside, the salad.
4. Mix the wasabi with a little water to form a paste. Wait 10 minutes for its pungency to develop and put a teaspoonful beside the fish in each of the plates or bowls.
5. Divide the soy sauce between four shallow bowls. Each diner mixes the wasabi to taste into the soy and dips in the fish slices lightly. If you are using ginger, peel the root and grate it into the soy sauce.

The Japanese are masters of the art of exquisite presentation. Learn how to carve a chrysanthemum as they do, from a white radish, or mooli.

Cut 6 × 4 cm (1½ inch) slices from a large white radish. Peel and trim the white radish slices into round turnip shapes. Hold the radish just above the base between a pair of chopsticks.

Slice the radish down thinly (the chopsticks will prevent you from slicing right through the base).

Turn at right angles and slice down thinly again. Sprinkle with salt, leave for 30-60 minutes, then drain and dry.

The radish will now be softened and easy to open out into a flower shape if you press lightly.

BAKED WHOLE SALMON

SERVES 8
1 whole salmon, about 1.75 kg (4 lb)
25 g (1 oz) butter
4 spring onions, trimmed
2 carrots, peeled and roughly chopped
a wedge of fennel
3 springs parsley
1 teaspoon dill weed
salt
whole black peppercorns
150 ml (¼ pint) white wine

Preparation time: about 15 minutes
Cooking time: about 20 minutes, plus cooling
Oven: 200°C, 400°F, Gas Mark 6

Whatever salmon farmers say, wild salmon does taste better. The idea of cooking whole fish often alarms people because they know they neither possess a fish kettle nor really want to. This method allows you to use your familiar roasting tin and ensures that the fish will stay moist. Serve salmon with hot new potatoes, hand-made mayonnaise and a cucumber salad dressed with rice vinegar (available from oriental supermarkets).

1. Ask the fishmonger to clean the salmon but leave on the head and the tail. At home check that any loose scales have been scraped off and give it a rinse in clear water.
2. Line a roasting tin with greaseproof paper, letting enough hang over the rim to provide a handle for lifting out the fish later. Smear the butter over the paper. Lay on the salmon and dot the vegetables, herbs and flavourings around.
3. Pour on the white wine and enough water to just come level with the fish. You may need to coil the fish to fit it in. Cover the pan with foil, pinching it well in around the sides. Put in the preheated oven and bring to a simmer. Simmer for 10 minutes. Remove.
5. Let cool and serve the fish, ideally lukewarm.

POACHED FISH BALLS WITH EGG AND LEMON SAUCE

450 g (1 lb) minced fish
2 egg whites
2 level tablespoons fine Matzoh meal
1 heaped teaspoon finely grated ginger root
1 heaped teaspoon finely chopped fresh parsley or coriander
salt
freshly ground black pepper

Stock
1 onion, peeled
1 carrot, peeled
½ teaspoon fennel seeds, or a piece of fennel root
a little lemon juice
a little white wine

Sauce
2 egg yolks
2 tablespoons lemon juice

Preparation time: about 20 minutes
Cooking time: about 20 minutes

One of the joys of minced fish is that it is quick to cook. Another is that it is relatively cheap; another that it is receptive to varied flavourings. Minced fish might strike you as an odd commodity, but in the part of North London where I live they sell it and, should you fail to find it, you can simply buy equal quantities of each of two kinds of white fish (no oily varieties) and chop them in a food processor or mincer. If you cannot find any Matzoh meal, use very fine breadcrumbs. I once made this for a Jewish friend on the grounds that it resembled gefilte fish. I don't think it does much, but he seemed to like it and said he was touched.

1. Add the stock ingredients to a large pan of water and bring to a simmer.
2. Mix the fish with the egg whites, Matzoh meal and seasonings, adding more meal, which has a binding but not ponderous effect, if necessary, to produce a consistency that can be formed into balls.
3. Using a dessertspoon, slide balls of the fish mixture into the water. Poach for about 10 minutes, never letting the water get much beyond a shudder.
4. Meanwhile, for the sauce, mix the egg yolks and half the lemon juice in a bowl. Remove 300 ml (½ pint) of stock from the pan. Whisk 2 tablespoons of it into the yolks. Pour the rest into a small heavy pan. Add the yolk mixture and stir over low heat until slightly thickened. Taste and add more lemon juice, if liked.
5. Remove the fish balls with a slotted spoon. Place in a warmed serving dish. Slice the carrot from the stock thinly and place a carrot round on each fish ball. Pour the sauce around, or serve separately.

ABOVE RIGHT: Baked whole salmon
BELOW RIGHT: Poached fish balls with egg and lemon sauce

COD WITH BACON AND MUSHROOMS

about 1 kg (2 lb) cod steaks
salt
freshly ground black pepper
a scraping of nutmeg
4–6 rashers lean back bacon
450 ml (3/4 pint) milk
225 g (8 oz) mushrooms, trimmed (peeled only if necessary), and sliced
25 g (1 oz) vegetable oil or butter, for frying
20 g (3/4 oz) butter
250 g (9 oz) flour
2 tablespoons double cream (optional)
2 tablespoons finely chopped fresh parsley

Preparation time: 5–10 minutes
Cooking time: about 35 minutes
Oven: 160°C, 325°F, Gas Mark 3

Cod and bacon are a good combination and this a quick and simple supper dish. I have never understood why cod is not more highly prized (could it be the name?) for the flavour is excellent and, just as important, the texture is appealing, with firmer flakes than you find with some of the classier species like halibut or turbot. Try to find cod steaks cut to a thickness of about 4 cm (1½ inches). Use back bacon and, if you can find them, field mushrooms.

1. Rub the cod with a little salt, pepper and nutmeg and arrange the steaks in a single layer in a shallow ovenproof dish not much bigger than the assembled pieces of fish.
2. Arrange the bacon on top. Pour on the milk – enough to come to a depth of about 2 cm (3/4 inch).
3. Bake for 30 minutes. While the cod is cooking fry the sliced mushrooms in oil or butter, according to preference.
4. Check the fish to see if it is cooked through. If so, remove it and the bacon to a warm serving dish.
5. In a small, heavy-bottomed pan, melt the 20 g (3/4 oz) butter, add the flour and stir well to make the basis of a roux. Use the fish-cooking milk to make a smooth sauce.
6. Finish it with cream if you are using it. Season with salt and pepper and sprinkle in the chopped parsley.
7. Pour the sauce round the fish and scatter on the fried mushrooms. Serve with plain boiled potatoes.

HERRINGS IN OATMEAL

4 fresh herrings
salt
freshly ground black pepper
50 g (2 oz) medium oatmeal
4 rashers back bacon

Mustard sauce:
2 egg yolks
2 teaspoons Dijon mustard
a little chopped fresh parsley
50 g (2 oz) butter

Preparation time: about 20 minutes
Cooking time: about 20 minutes

ABOVE LEFT: Cod with bacon and mushrooms
BELOW LEFT: Herrings in oatmeal

When dwelling on the subject of herrings, which I hope you will for a minute, it would be salutary to think about what has happened to oysters. Once so plentiful that herrings were considered food for the poor, now they are prized and extremely pricey. One herring apparently lays at least ten thousand eggs and so you would think they were exempt from the fate of the oyster, but over-fishing has already affected the shoals and so one day they, too, may join the ranks of luxury ingredients. Before they do, cook them in this homely but delicious manner. A further incentive might be the fact that herrings are very good for you. It is not only the highly unsaturated oil. They feed on plankton, full of nutrients. As one cookery book puts it, 'The herring, like most fish, are the cattle of a vegetation other than our own'.

1. Slit the herrings along their bellies and clean them out. Skin side up, press firmly on the back-bone. Turn the fish over. You should be able easily to pick off the bones, rather like undoing a zip.
2. Season them well. Press them into the oatmeal until they are well coated.
3. Fry the bacon gently until the fat runs, then fry the fish in the bacon fat (you may need extra oil) until they are crisp on both sides. Season.
4. Serve the fish and bacon together (the flavours marry well) with mustard sauce.
5. In a bowl mix the egg yolks and mustard and chopped parsley, if available. Melt the butter gently. When it is just melted, not madly hot, stir it into the yolks as if making mayonnaise. Use immediately – a very useful little sauce.

LEG OF MONKFISH

SERVES 4–6

1 tail of monkfish, weighing about 1–1.5 kg (2–3 lb)
2 cloves garlic, peeled and cut into strips
4 tablespoons good olive oil
4 tomatoes, peeled and sliced
1 onion, peeled and cut into fine crescents
1 teaspoon fennel seeds (optional)
1 small lemon, sliced
200 ml (7 fl oz) white wine
salt
freshly ground black pepper
chopped fresh parsley

Preparation time: about 10 minutes
Cooking time: 35–40 minutes
Oven: 220°C, 425°F, Gas Mark 7

I suspect that there are few discoveries left to be made about cooking. There was a time when monkfish (otherwise known as angler) went unappreciated in this country and was therefore relatively cheap. Now it is every restaurateur's darling, not least of all because its firm flesh is claimed by some to resemble lobster. The tail of monkfish vaguely resembles the shape of a leg of lamb and the French often serve it roasted, as a 'gigot de lotte'. Prepared this way it will convert anyone who thinks fish is sissy.

1. Skin the fish scrupulously, removing all the membrane, which, if left, will cause the fish to curl up in the oven.
2. With a sharp knife, slip the chips of garlic into the flesh, dotting it about until the surface is fairly well covered. Tie at intervals with string, to help the fish keep its shape.
3. Heat the olive oil in an ovenproof dish and brown the fish lightly.
4. Scatter around the fish the tomatoes, onion, fennel seeds and lemon slices. Pour the white wine over the fish. Season thoroughly.
5. Cook in the pre-heated oven, basting from time to time with the pan juice, for 35–40 minutes.
6. Serve on a heated plate with the mixture from the pan poured around. Sprinkle with chopped parsley.

INDIAN BARBECUED FISH

2 teaspoons ground coriander
2 teaspoons ground cumin
½ teaspoon turmeric
1 teaspoon cinnamon
1 teaspoon fennel seeds
1 teaspoon black onion seeds (kalonji) (optional)
1 onion, peeled and roughly chopped
4 cloves garlic
2.5 cm (1 inch) square peeled piece fresh ginger root (more if you like the flavour)
1 small green chilli, seeded, or pinch of chilli powder
3 tablespoons lemon juice
300 ml (½ pint) plain yogurt
salt
freshly ground black pepper
1 kg (2 lb) fish; choose either one large fish, several smaller fish or fish steaks e.g. cod

Preparation time: 15–20 minutes, plus marinading
Cooking time: about 10–15 minutes

This spicy barbecue sauce is particularly good with fish, but it could also be used with chicken. If so, the meat should be allowed to marinate in it for longer. The optimum way of cooking the fish is over charcoal, but if this is not practical just line a grill pan with foil and cook the fish under the grill. The spices given below need not be adhered to meticulously; they are a guideline. If the array of individual spices seems daunting, use 1 level tablespoon garam masala from a recently purchased tin. To save time, make the marinade in the morning, and leave the fish marinading in the refrigerator until ready to cook.

1. Grind the spices if you are starting with them in their whole form.
2. In a liquidizer or food processor whizz together the onion, peeled garlic cloves, peeled ginger root roughly chopped, fresh chilli, lemon juice and 2 tablespoons of the yogurt.
3. Add the rest of the yogurt and spices, season with salt and pepper and blend again.
4. Cut slits in the body of whole fish. Rub the marinade into the fish, both inside and out for whole fish, and leave covered by the rest of the marinade for about 2 hours.
5. Shake off the excess marinade and grill over a medium heat until the flesh is opaque and the skin crisps. One of those sort of sandwich-shaped metal contraptions makes grilling fish on a barbecue much more satisfactory.
6. Season. Serve with lemon quarters, onion rings and, if possible, chopped fresh coriander.

ABOVE RIGHT: Leg of monkfish
BELOW RIGHT: Indian barbecued fish

GRAVAD LAX

SERVES 4–6
1 piece of salmon, either a tail-piece or a whole small salmon or salmon trout, weighing 750 g–1 kg (1½–2 lb)
1 heaped tablespoon sea salt
1 rounded tablespoon sugar
1 teaspoon coarsely ground black pepper
a little brandy (optional)
1 rounded tablespoon fresh dill, chopped

Sauce:
mayonnaise, preferably home-made
German mustard
sugar
dill
dash of vinegar

Preparation time: 5 minutes, plus marinading

This Scandinavian treatment of fish, usually salmon, which involves marinating it in a mixture of sugar and salt, had a great vogue in restaurants some years back. It appealed to customers as a diverting change from smoked salmon and, because it was foreign, seemed glamorous. For these reasons restaurateurs seemed to feel it was perfectly all right to charge a price quite out of proportion to that of the raw material or the work involved. The preparation takes only a few minutes. The sugar and salt pickle works well on humbler fish such as herring, but the first time try a tail piece of salmon, a cut sometimes sold a little more cheaply than the main body of the fish.

1. Bone the fish which will give you two kite-shaped pieces, or, if you have bought a small salmon or salmon trout, clean, bone and behead it. Ask the fishmonger to do this if you are unsure about it. You can also remove the skin now and use it as a wrapping around the fish while it is marinating, spreading the seasoning between the skin and the fish.
2. Mix together the salt, sugar and pepper. If you wish, moisten with a little brandy.
3. Put some of this pickle mixture plus a third of the dill into a dish that holds the fish quite snugly, lay on it the first piece of fish, skin side down.
4. Spread on more pickle, more dill and sandwich with the other piece of fish, skin side up. Scatter on the remaining pickle and dill.
5. Cover with a double layer of aluminium foil and then weight down with tins or a brick. Leave in the fridge for at least 24 hours, turning once.
6. To serve, remove the skin, slice thinly and drain off the brine. Mix together the ingredients for the sauce. Hand round rye bread or accompany with boiled new potatoes, and serve with the sauce.

MACKEREL WITH GOOSEBERRY SAUCE

SERVES 2
100 g (4 oz) butter
1 tablespoon chopped fresh parsley
2 tablespoons lemon juice
1 teaspoon Dijon mustard
2 mackerel, gutted and washed

Sauce:
450 g (1 lb) gooseberries
25 g (1 oz) butter
sugar, to taste
1 egg or 3 tablespoons double cream

Preparation time: about 15 minutes
Cooking time: about 15 minutes

ABOVE LEFT: Gravad lax
BELOW LEFT: Mackerel with gooseberry sauce

Mackerel are supposed to be food for your heart. Eat mackerel often and the fishy oils therein will protect you from attack.

Buy fish that can look you straight in the eye and are almost iridescent in colour. Grill them without fudging the first blast of heat which gives a crisp skin. A mackerel weighing about 500 g (1 lb) will feed two as a first course, one as a main course.

1. Make the grilling butter by mixing together 75 g (3 oz) of butter, the parsley, lemon juice and mustard.
2. Prepare the sauce: Top and tail the gooseberries. Melt 25 g (1 oz) butter in a heavy-bottomed pan and add the gooseberries. Cover and cook gently until they fall apart and are cooked through. Taste for tartness and add sugar if you wish, but take care not to over-sweeten.
3. Either mash, sieve or whizz in a food processor and then stir in the egg, beaten, or the cream.
4. Make your grill very hot. With a sharp knife make three diagonal slashes on the mackerel down to the bone. Work a little parsley butter into each slash.
5. Grill for a minute and then reduce the heat somewhat. After 4 minutes, baste the fish with the melted butter in the grill pan.
6. When the fish is opaque, turn over and repeat the slashing, anointing and grilling process.
7. Serve the fish with the sauce handed separately and the remaining parsley butter as a pat on top of the fish.

POULTRY AND GAME

Forget the upmarket image of game, and enjoy the special taste of Quails with Rice or Normandy Pheasant – a far cry from battery birds. Rabbit, too, is coming back into fashion. Try the Italian version here, with its scents of olive oil, garlic and thyme. For roast chicken in a hurry, try Spatchcocked Chicken, flattened, seasoned and grilled to produce the perfect speedy supper.

Duck breasts with apples

NORMANDY PHEASANT

SERVES 2–3
50 g (2 oz) butter
1 tablespoon vegetable oil
1 plump pheasant
2 dessert apples, peeled, cored and sliced
2 tablespoons Calvados or 300 ml (½ pint) cider, reduced by vigorous boiling to 2 tablespoons
300 ml (½ pint) double cream or 150 ml (¼ pint) double cream and 1 Petit Suisse or some fromage blanc
salt
freshly ground black pepper

Preparation time: about 10 minutes
Cooking time: about 1 hour
Oven: 190°C, 375°F, Gas Mark 5

1. In half the butter and the oil, sauté the trussed pheasant (without its pork back fat, if any) until golden on all sides. Remove from the pan and in the remaining butter and other pan juices gently fry the apples slices.
2. Find an earthenware casserole, or similar ovenproof dish with a lid, which will hold the pheasant quite snugly. Place the apples in the bottom, the pheasant on them. Add the Calvados or cider to the pan juices, bubble them for a minute or two and then pour them on the pheasant. Cover the bird and cook in the oven for approximately 30 minutes.
3. Remove the casserole from the oven, and add the cream. If you are wanting to use less cream for health reasons, do as the French do and put the Petit Suisse cheese or fromage blanc inside the bird and pour in the smaller amount of cream.
4. Season with salt and freshly ground black pepper. Take the opportunity to turn the pheasant over so that it is breast side down. Return the casserole to the oven for another 15 minutes.
5. Serve the bird on a warm dish. Stir the sauce until well amalgamated, reducing if necessary by boiling for added thickness. Pour it around the pheasant.

RABBIT AS I REMEMBER IT IN ITALY

4 tablespoons olive oil
175 g (6 oz) belly pork or bacon, cubed
1 onion or 3 shallots, peeled and chopped
1 young rabbit, jointed, or 1 kg (2 lb) frozen rabbit, defrosted
2–3 garlic cloves, peeled and slivered
200 ml (7 fl oz) red wine
1 × 400 g (14 oz) can peeled tomatoes or carton of sieved tomatoes
2 tablespoons tomato paste
2-3 tablespoons lemon juice
1 scant dessertspoon dried oregano or thyme
a good pinch of brown sugar
salt
freshly ground black pepper
a tiny pinch of chilli powder or red pepper flakes

Garnish:
chopped fresh parsley
slices of French bread rubbed with garlic and toasted in the oven

Preparation time: about 10 minutes
Cooking time: about 1¼ hours

The Italians and the French approach rabbit with considerably more enthusiasm than do the British, who seem lastingly haunted by the spectre of myxomatosis. Those dire days now long gone; it is time to appreciate the mildly gamy, lean flavour of rabbit, invariably more interesting than chicken. Soho butchers often have rabbits, tame and wild, hanging in their shop windows and they will skin them for you. If you buy a wild rabbit, get a small young one. Enterprising supermarkets sell frozen rabbit, much of it coming from China. Do not give it to the cat; follow the recipe below, which is as close as I can come to emulating a dish of rabbit I ate in a country inn in Italy. The sauce had an almost jammy consistency and the scent of olive oil and wild thyme beckoned. Indeed, if you are sure you have a tender rabbit, the creature is also excellent simply roasted in the oven with those two flavourings plus garlic. A particularly robust chicken could be substituted for rabbit in this dish. If short of time make this dish the day before, reheat and finish off the sauce just before serving.

1. In half the olive oil sauté the pork or bacon until the fat begins to run. Add the onion or shallots and stir until softened. Add the rabbit and the garlic and sauté, turning, until the meat is lightly browned.
2. Add the wine, bubble up and reduce it a little. Add the tomatoes, tomato paste, lemon juice, the remaining olive oil and the herbs and seasonings.
3. Simmer, uncovered, until the meat is tender, up to an hour, depending on the youth of the rabbit. When tender, remove to a warm serving dish.
4. Reduce the sauce until it is thick and shiny and only enough to coat the meat meanly. Taste for seasoning.
5. Pour the sauce on the rabbit. Sprinkle with parsley and serve with the toasted bread.

ABOVE RIGHT: Normandy pheasant
BELOW RIGHT: Rabbit as I remember it in Italy

SPATCHCOCKED CHICKEN

4 poussins or 2 small (spring) chickens
juice of ½ lemon
2 fat garlic cloves, peeled and crushed
salt
freshly ground black pepper
½ teaspoon cayenne pepper
1 tablespoon olive oil
25 g (1 oz) butter
1 tablespoon Dijon mustard
2 tablespoons dried breadcrumbs (not orange packet crumbs)

Preparation time: about 20 minutes
Cooking time: about 25 minutes

This recipe makes it possible to grill rather than roast a small bird and when you take trouble with the seasoning it is a perfect speedy supper. I suggest a watercress salad as an accompaniment as I think watercress and chicken go well together. Dress the leaves simply by pouring on the hot juices from the grill pan.

1. Using poultry shears, cut the chickens along the backbone, the underside of the bird. Spread out and flatten completely by pressing down firmly on the backbone until you hear it crack. Be quite sadistic.
2. Rub the top side of the chickens with lemon juice and then with the crushed garlic. Season with salt, black pepper and the cayenne pepper. Dribble some of the oil over the chickens and then dot with half the butter.
3. Turn the grill to moderately high. Grill the prepared chickens, breast side up, for about 10 minutes. Turn over, season again, and anoint with the remaining oil and butter. Cook for another 10 minutes.
4. Turn the chickens back, breast side up, and paint with the mustard. Sprinkle on the breadcrumbs and put back under the grill until the crumbs are crisp. Serve on hot plates with the salad described in the introduction above – or, whatever you fancy.

DUCK BREASTS WITH APPLES

SERVES 2
2 duck breasts
salt
freshly ground pepper
a little ground ginger
25 g (1 oz) butter
1 dessert apple, peeled, cored and cut into crescents
4 tablespoons apple juice
1 tablespoon green peppercorns in brine, drained well (optional)

Preparation time: about 10 minutes
Cooking time: 15–20 minutes

ABOVE LEFT: Spatchcocked chicken
BELOW LEFT: Duck breasts with apples

Although *magret de canard,* the style in which duck breasts so often appears on menus, no longer tempts me to order it in restaurants, it makes an ideal quick and luxurious meal at home. The idea below is adapted from a recipe of Anton Mosimann. You could also make use of fruit canned without syrup, such as blackcurrants, blueberries or blackberries, to make a sauce that you pep up with red wine, freshly ground black pepper and any meat juices from cooking the duck, and thicken with 1½ teaspoons arrowroot first mixed into a little of the liquid, then returned to the sauce.

1. Vigorously season the duck breasts on both sides with salt, pepper and ginger. Make your grill and grill pan red hot and place on it the duck, skin side down in order to brand the skin.
2. Lower the heat to medium and turn the meat over. Cook 5–6 minutes, turn again and cook until the meat *just* loses its pink; in all about 10–12 minutes.
3. While this is going on, melt the butter in a small pan. Add the apple slices and cook gently. After they are glazed, pour in the apple juice, add the peppercorns if you are using them, and bubble the juice until slightly reduced.
4. Serve the duck breasts, either as they are or sliced across the grain and fanned out, with the apples and the sauce poured around.

QUAILS WITH INTERESTING RICE

8 quails
½ lemon
spices (ground coriander or cumin, cardamom, ginger, black pepper)
225 g (8 oz) basmati rice
50 g (2 oz) butter
300 ml (½ pint) light stock, or water
1 tablespoon vegetable oil
100 g (4 oz) sausage meat
1 small round lettuce, trimmed and cut across into thin ribbons
120 ml (4 fl oz) cream (if you want to make a sauce)

Preparation time: about 15 minutes
Cooking time: about 25 minutes

Quails are often sold in packets of six. You will need at least two quails per person.

This is a very pretty assembly. I have served it with success at parties and it has the added advantage of being quick to cook. If you don't have the spices mentioned in the recipe, don't fret. Use what is to hand but remember that quails need a bit of gingering up, as they are farmed birds. Sometimes I use the pan juices plus cream to make a small amount of sauce to dribble over the birds.

1. Rub the quails with the lemon and then with a mixture of the ground spices. Let them sit absorbing these flavours.
2. Wash the rice well to remove any clinging starch and then either sauté it first in 25 g (1 oz) of melted butter and add enough light stock to cook, or cook in water, according to preference.
3. About 15 minutes before the rice is ready, heat the oil and the rest of the butter and sauté the spiced quails, first turning them until evenly browned and then cooking them over a gentle heat until all traces of pink in the flesh are gone.
4. In a separate pan fry the sausage meat, breaking it up with a fork until it resembles crumbs. Mix the cooked rice with the sausage meat and the lettuce, folding it in sensitively.
5. Arrange the quails on top. If you want to make a sauce, add cream to the pan juices and heat the mixture gently to avoid curdling.

CHICKEN WINGS WITH CHICK PEAS

3 tablespoons vegetable oil
2 onions, peeled and finely sliced
2 garlic cloves, peeled and crushed
4 cm (1½ inch) piece of fresh ginger root, or ½ teaspoon powdered ginger (but that is less good)
1 teaspoon cumin seeds or powdered cumin
½ teaspoon cardamom seeds, taken from their husks
1 teaspoon coriander seeds or ground coriander
12-15 chicken wings
about 600 ml (1 pint) light chicken stock
2 × 400 g (14 oz) cans chickpeas, well drained
salt
freshly ground black pepper
2 tablespoons lime or lemon juice
natural yogurt, to serve (optional)

Preparation time: about 10 minutes
Cooking time: 30–35 minutes

Of all the bits of chicken that are sold separately, I like the wings the best, but then I like skin and bones and joints and cartilage – and not too much meat. Marinated in garlic and lime juice and grilled until they crisp, they accompany well a drink, or some green salad, or both. Lebanese restaurants are adept at preparing spiced and grilled chicken wings. The recipe below produces a more substantial meal, one that I observe finds favour with children who like the licence to pick food up in their fingers. They can even be persuaded to see the point of chickpeas. I have suggested canned chickpeas in the interest of speed. You could, of course, soak dried chickpeas overnight and then boil them for an hour or two, but chickpeas are so nobly resilient that the canning process makes little impact.

1. In a sauté pan or frying pan large enough to hold the wings more or less in one layer, heat the oil to a medium heat. Sauté the onions until they are softened. Add the garlic, ginger which you have rubbed through a grater, and the spices. Stir around to cook, without catching, for about 3 minutes.
2. Make sure the chicken wings are free of any stubble (cut off the wing tips, if necessary). Add them to the spiced oil. Cook, turning and shifting them about until they are browned.
3. Add the stock. Bubble up and then add the chickpeas.
4. Simmer uncovered, but continually turning the wings until they are cooked and the sauce is reduced. Season.
5. Sprinkle with lemon or lime juice and serve. Plain unsweetened yogurt sits well alongside this.

ABOVE RIGHT: Quails with interesting rice
BELOW RIGHT: Chicken wings with chick peas

MEAT

Why does Toad in the Clouds sound so much more appealing than toad in the hole? Here, the humble hamburger is transformed by the American salt-grilled method, while Sweet and Sour Pork or Szechuan Bean Curd are both easy and exotic. For a more robust treat, try Bistecca, which takes very little effort.

Roast stuffed fillet of pork

SWEET AND SOUR PORK

3 pork cutlets or 350 g (12 oz) pork fillet
1 dessertspoon soy sauce
1 fat garlic clove, peeled and crushed
1 egg, beaten
vegetable oil for deep-frying
2 tablespoons cornflour
1 onion, peeled and finely chopped

Sauce:
2 tablespoons potato flour
4 tablespoons water
4 tablespoons pineapple or apple juice
2 tablespoons wine vinegar
3 tablespoons sugar
2 teaspoons soy sauce
2 tablespoons tomato ketchup
2 teaspoons Worcestershire sauce

Preparation time: about 25 minutes
Cooking time: about 30 minutes

From time to time in Chinese restaurants, particularly when I have my children in tow, I order sweet and sour pork to see if it can be good. Wanting to disguise some pork cutlets the other evening for children who think grilled meat is boring, I chopped them up and made them according to the recipe below. The cubes of meat were excellent, crisp outside and moist and flavourful inside, and the sauce, rather to my astonishment, received great acclaim from the children as being almost identical to that you get in restaurants.

1. Chop the meat into 2.5 cm (1 inch) cubes. Put in a bowl with the soy sauce and garlic and turn to coat well.
2. Meanwhile, mix together the sauce ingredients, stirring the liquids and then the sugar and sauces into the potato flour.
3. Add the beaten egg to the meat and stir again.
4. Heat the oil in a wok or deep-fryer to a depth that will cover the meat (a bit of swirling about means you can use less oil). Roll each meat cube in cornflour and assemble them on a plate.
5. When the oil is chip-frying hot, add the meat and cook until the outside is crisp and lightly browned. Drain the meat on kitchen paper.
6. Fry the onion in a little fresh oil. Add the sauce mixture and bring to a simmer. It will thicken and shine.
7. Repeat the meat frying for a minute or two only. Add a little more oil to the sauce, which will obviate any glueyness.
8. Serve the meat on boiled rice with some sauce trickled over and the rest served separately for real enthusiasts.

FEUILLETÉ OF KIDNEYS

450 g (1 lb) lamb's or calf's kidneys
225 g (8 oz) frozen puff pastry or 1 large vol-au-vent case
50 g (2 oz) butter
2–3 shallots, or 1 onion, peeled and finely chopped
1 garlic clove, peeled and finely slivered
1 tablespoon sherry vinegar or wine vinegar
a splash of Madeira or port (optional)
150 ml (¼ pint) chicken stock
1 egg yolk
2 tablespoons double cream
1 generous dessertspoon Dijon mustard
salt
freshly ground black pepper

Preparation time: about 15 minutes
Cooking time: 35–40 minutes
Oven: 200–230°C, 400–450°F, Gas Mark 6–8, or according to packet instructions

Feuilleté is a popular word on restaurant menus these days. It means puff pastry and a receptacle which can enable a restaurateur to 'stretch' a relatively small amount of whatever ingredient becomes the filling, be it seafood or meat.

1. Preheat the oven according to pastry instructions on the packet. Trim the kidneys of any gristle or membrane and winkle out the fatty core. Leave lamb kidneys whole. Slice the veal kidneys into 6–12 mm (¼–½ inch) slices.
2. While you cook your puff pastry in the shape you fancy, round or oblong, and according to packet instructions, start on the kidneys and sauce.
3. Melt the butter and gently sauté the kidneys for about 5 minutes. You want them to stay a little pink at their heart. Remove them and keep warm.
4. Sauté the shallots or onion and garlic until softened. When the shallot or onion and garlic mixture is golden add the vinegar and bubble fiercely (a splash of Madeira or port improves matters). Add the stock and simmer for about 15 minutes.
5. Beat the egg yolk and cream in a small bowl. Add 2 tablespoons of the stock to the egg mixture. Return this, well mixed, to the sauce and cook over a low heat until it is thickened. Stir in the mustard and season. Heat through.
6. Slice the kidneys if they are whole and warm them through in the sauce. Sandwich between the pastry or spoon into the vol-au-vent case.

ABOVE RIGHT: Sweet and sour pork
BELOW RIGHT: Feuilleté of kidneys

PORK IN LETTUCE WRAP

2 tablespoons vegetable oil or lard, according to preference
350 g (12 oz) minced pork
a pinch of salt
1 teaspoon sugar
1 tablespoon chopped onion
1 teaspoon grated fresh ginger root
4 celery sticks, stringed and diced
1 tablespoon soy sauce
2 tablespoons dry sherry
about 85 ml (3 fl oz) chicken stock (from a cube will suffice)
½ cucumber, diced
½ tablespoon cornflour
2 teaspoons sesame oil or other vegetable oil (optional)
1 iceberg or Webb's lettuce, the leaves separated, washed and dried

Preparation time: about 10 minutes
Cooking time: about 25 minutes

Wrapping things in lettuce leaves is all the go in Chinese restaurants these days. Quite often the menu will claim that the substance to be wrapped is minced quail or squab (young pigeon), but in reality it is most likely to be pork, as below. One of the advantages of this mode of eating, alongside the illusion of healthiness, is the involving quality of the activity, which therefore makes it a good dinner party dish if you are a bit short on conversation. This is a somewhat simplified version of a Chinese recipe, but once you have got the hang of it you will think of your own mixtures.

1. Heat the oil or lard (the latter gives a more unctuous effect) in a large frying pan or wok. When hot, add the pork. Sprinkle with a good pinch of salt and the sugar, and stir-fry for 2–3 minutes, or until there is no trace of pink in the meat.
2. Add the onion and ginger and stir-fry for 2 minutes. Add the celery, soy sauce, sherry and 3 tablespoons of the stock. Fry for a minute, then add the cucumber and cook until it is heated through but still crunchy.
3. Whisk the cornflour into the remaining stock, give it a stir to create a cloudy liquid, and pour on to the meat. Stir-fry for a minute.
4. Finally, glaze the meat by dribbling on the sesame oil or a little vegetable oil, if that is all you have to hand.
5. Serve on a heated dish with the lettuce leaves stacked on a separate plate. Each person takes a leaf, spoons in the pork mixture, makes a parcel and eats.

BISTECCA ALLA FIORENTINA

SERVES 2
1 garlic clove, peeled and halved (optional)
2 steaks, such as T-bone, rump or sirloin, but at least 2.5 cm (1 inch) thick
a little olive oil
salt
freshly ground black pepper
lemon wedges

Preparation time: about 10 minutes
Cooking time: about 5 minutes

ABOVE LEFT: Pork in lettuce wrap
BELOW LEFT: Bistecca alla Fiorentina

Meat grilled over the fire is a speciality of Florence and the key to success is a well-hung piece of steak, a hot fire and little interference otherwise. Since a fragrant wood fire is hard for most of us to arrange, I am instead going to quote from some notes of an American friend of mine on the cooking of a perfect steak which requires instead a heavy-based, preferably cast-iron, frying pan. 'To achieve the best from the meat, one tries to cook in such a manner that it is charred almost black on the outside and remains red (or just barely turning to pink) in the centre. All well-grilled or roasted beef ideally should have this range from black to red in each mouthful. If you say you don't care for it that way, you actually don't care to get the best from the taste of beef, so why bother to pay the extravagant price?'

1. Put the frying pan, which should not be a flimsy affair, on the hob and turn on the gas or electricity to maximum. Leave the pan on for about 5 minutes until it seems almost red hot.
2. If you like the flavour of garlic rub the surface of the meat with a cut clove before grilling. Now drop in the steaks without butter, oil or seasoning (seasoning before cooking toughens the meat).
3. Turn the meat after 2 minutes, using a spatula or tongs or wooden spoons; you want to avoid piercing it. Rub the cooked side with a little olive oil. Cook the other side until it, too, has a dark crust.
4. Season after cooking and serve on heated plates (otherwise the surface temperature of the steak will fall fast). Garnish with lemon wedges.

SZECHUAN BEAN CURD

3 tablespoons Chinese dried shrimps
4 medium dried mushrooms
1½ tablespoons salted black beans
2 dried chillies or 1 fresh chilli
5 tablespoons vegetable oil
1 onion, peeled and sliced
2 garlic cloves, peeled and slivered
a pinch of salt
225 g (8 oz) minced pork or beef
a splash of soy sauce
2 teaspoons cornflour mixed with 8 tablespoons stock
3 cakes bean curd
a few spring onions, trimmed and finely chopped

Preparation time: 30 minutes
Cooking time: about 30 minutes

Although I know, as no doubt do you, that bean curd is the most sane form of protein, I have been nervous of cooking it. I was impressed therefore, when lunching with a friend, to see her turning cubes of bean curd in wholemeal flour and frying them to a reasonably crispy consistency and then adding some stir-fried vegetables. It made a good meal. If you want a non-meat meal, the minced pork or beef could be omitted.

1. Soak the shrimps and mushrooms in warm water for 30 minutes. Drain and chop, pushing aside the mushroom stems.
2. Soak the black beans in water for a few minutes. Drain. Finely chop the chillies, discarding the seeds. You might want less chilli if you dislike fiery food.
3. Heat 4 tablespoons of the oil in a frying pan or wok. Add the onion, garlic and a pinch of salt. Stir-fry for a few minutes.
4. Add the chillies, shrimps and mushrooms and stir-fry for 2 minutes. Add the mince and black beans and cook until the meat is browned. Add a splash of soy sauce. Simmer the mixture for 5 minutes.
5. Pour in the blended cornflour. Bring to the boil. Stir until the mixture thickens. Remove from the heat.
5. Slice the bean curd. Quickly fry in the remaining oil until golden on both sides.
6. Add the bean curd. Heat through carefully. Serve in a bowl with the spring onions sprinkled on top and some boiled rice.

CORNED BEEF HASH

450 g (1 lb) can corned beef
750 g (1½ lbs) boiled potatoes, cubed
1 large onion, peeled and finely chopped
freshly ground black pepper
Worcestershire sauce, Tabasco or chilli sauce, to taste
25 g (1 oz) butter
2–3 tablespoons vegetable oil
1 egg per person (optional)

Preparation time: 10 minutes
Cooking time: 15–20 minutes

This recipe may seem, how shall we say, artless, but it is a good short-order dish, possible often to assemble from what you have in your stores. The important factors about corned beef hash are a crisp crust on the bottom, an enlivening ingredient such as a splash of Tabasco, Worcestershire sauce or chilli sauce and, arguably, one fried egg for each person perched on top. It is ideal for leftover boiled potatoes, but if you are cooking them just for this dish make them slightly underdone.

1. Open can of corned beef carefully (apparently horrible accidents are caused every year by fumble-fingers with the corned beef tin). Break up the meat and, in a bowl, mix it with the potatoes and onion. If you prefer, you can fry the onion first until it is limp and beginning to brown. Season the mixture with pepper and Worcestershire sauce.
2. Melt the butter in a frying pan with the vegetable oil. When hot, add the hash mixture and press down firmly. When a crust begins to form on the bottom, turn the mixture to bring some crust to the top and to allow a new one to form. Cook slowly until you are satisfied there is enough crust.
3. Turn out on to a hot plate and divide into four. Serve each portion with a fried egg on top if you fancy that.

ABOVE RIGHT: Szechuan bean curd
BELOW RIGHT: Corned beef hash

大核貸款一億美元
國際銀行爭取參與

LIVER VENEZIANA

750 g (1½ lb) calf's liver, sliced 5 mm (¼ inch) thick
3 tablespoons vegetable oil
6 medium onions, peeled and thinly sliced
salt
freshly ground pepper
frisé lettuce, to garnish

Preparation time: about 10 minutes
Cooking time: about 25 minutes

It is important to start with good calf's liver and to find a butcher who will slice it evenly and thinly. You want the slices about 5 mm (¼ inch) thick. The onions may be cooked ahead of time, but it is important that they, too, should be carefully cooked – browned but not scorched. Italian mashed potatoes, pureed and beaten with hot milk, butter or olive oil and grated Parmesan cheese, is a fine accompaniment.

1. Pick over the liver and cut away any skin, gristle or tubes. Cut the liver into pieces about the size of a visiting card.
2. Heat the oil in a large frying pan large enough to hold the liver slices in one layer, and sauté the sliced onions over a gentle heat for about 15 minutes or until soft and golden brown. Remove the onions with a slotted spoon, leaving the oil behind. Keep the onions warm.
3. Turn the heat right up and, when the oil is very hot, add the liver. As soon as the liver loses its raw colour, turn it. Add salt and freshly ground pepper and, a few seconds later, the onions.
4. Give everything one more turn and serve immediately on a warm dish. If cut in the right way, the liver should cook in less than a minute and be as tender as butter. Garnish with a little frisé.

ROAST STUFFED FILLET OF PORK

1 pork fillet
1 long, thin spicy fresh sausage
2 bacon rashers
3–4 bay leaves
salt
freshly ground black pepper
red wine, as required

Preparation time: about 20 minutes
Cooking time: 45 minutes
Oven: 190°C, 375°F, Gas Mark 5
Microwave time: about 16 minutes, plus standing

ABOVE LEFT: Liver Veneziana
BELOW LEFT: Roast stuffed fillet of pork

A letter from a butcher pointed out that customers – and butchers – are often confused by the various terms for meat. By fillet of pork I mean the long, lean, cylindrical cut usually sold in one piece. Sometimes it is called tenderloin.

If pressed for time you could stuff and tie the pork the day before and store in the freezer overnight.

1. With a sharp knife, score the fillet twice lengthways, spacing the cuts evenly and making sure you don't cut right through the meat – just about halfway down. You can now flatten it out into an oblong shape by banging with a mallet or another suitable blunt instrument.
2. Trim the sausage to the length of the meat and lay it down the middle. Wrap the meat round the sausage. Lay the bacon pieces along the join and tie in several places to make a neat parcel. Tuck some bay leaves under the string. Season with a little salt and a lot of freshly ground black pepper.
3. Place the meat in a roasting pan, surround it with cheap red wine and cook in the preheated oven for about 45 minutes, checking occasionally that the wine has not completely evaporated and adding more wine as necessary. You should finish with about a cupful of sauce.
4. Remove the string before slicing.

MICROWAVE

If short of time, this dish can be cooked in the microwave: Preheat the combination microwave oven to 190°C. Follow steps 1 and 2, then place the meat in a roasting dish, surround it with red wine and combination bake at 190°C on Full (100%) power for 3½ minutes. Reduce the power level to Medium (50%) and combination bake for a further 12–14 minutes, checking from time to time that the wine has not completely evaporated and adding more wine, stock or water as necessary. You should finish with about a cupful of sauce. Leave to stand, covered, for 5–10 minutes before carving.

SALT-GRILLED HAMBURGER

SERVES 2
225 g (8 oz) minced beef (not too lean as some fat is desirable)
1 small onion, peeled and finely chopped
1 egg yolk
1 garlic clove, peeled and crushed
1 teaspoon soy sauce
freshly ground black pepper
a handful of sea salt

Sauce (alternative method):
15 g (½ oz) butter
1 teaspoon olive oil
1 dessertspoon flour
milk, as required
1 tablespoon cream (optional)

Preparation time: about 10 minutes
Cooking time: 10–15 minutes

An American friend taught me how to make this hamburger. Perhaps since, in the interests of their blood pressure, Americans no longer eat salt, they feel that flinging it in the pan doesn't count. What it achieves is a nice crust on the meat and a virtuous, salt-free centre. A good hamburger is something not to be despised. Because you can flavour it in fairly ingenious ways it strikes me as more interesting to eat than a steak and is, of course, considerably cheaper.

As an alternative, you can cook the hamburgers with a quick 'pan gravy' as the Americans call it. However, in that case abandon the salt-grilling method as it would make the sauce unpalatable.

1. Using your hands, mix the beef with the onion, egg yolk, garlic, soy sauce and some pepper. Form into two hamburgers.
2. Scatter the sea salt in a heavy bottomed frying pan. Place on the stove and when hot cook the hamburgers (with no fat) until brown and crusty on the outside but a little pink inside.
3. To make the hamburgers with the sauce, add a little salt to the beef mixture and fry the burgers in a mixture of butter and olive oil. When cooked, remove the burgers and keep them warm.
4. Stir the flour into the fat and meat juices in the pan until well amalgamated and lightly brown. Slowly stir in milk, until you have a sauce the consistency of double cream and free of lumps (sieve, if necessary).
5. Taste for seasoning and if you are using cream, stir it in. Serve the burgers with this 'pan gravy'.

TOAD IN THE CLOUDS

450 g (1 lb) pork sausages
260 ml (8½ fl oz) milk
50 g (2 oz) butter and more to grease dish
150 g (5 oz) self-raising flour, sifted
4 eggs
2 large tomatoes, skinned and each cut into 8 crescents
salt
freshly ground black pepper
mustard, as required
a little top of the milk, or thin cream
50 g (2 oz) Cheddar cheese, diced

Preparation time: about 20 minutes
Cooking time: 50–55 minutes
Oven: 220°C, 425°F, Gas Mark 7
Microwave time: about 28 minutes

For this dish choose sausages with a high meat content and a mustard that has a good zing to it.

1. Skin the sausages and divide each one lengthways into two.
2. Put the milk into a large heavy saucepan. Cut the butter into it in flakes. Set on the heat, allowing the butter to melt by the time the milk has reached boiling point. At this stage tip in the sifted flour. Let the milk seethe up over it. Remove from the heat and allow to cool for a few minutes. Beat in the eggs.
3. Butter a 25 cm (10 inch) diameter soufflé dish. Cover the base with some of the batter. Arrange the sausages on the top, with the tomatoes tucked in between. Season with salt and pepper and spread the sausages lightly with mustard.
4. Cover with remaining batter, making sure the sausages and tomatoes are completely covered. Brush the surface with milk or cream. Sprinkle with the cheese.
5. Bake near the top of the preheated oven for about 40–45 minutes.

MICROWAVE
Preheat the combination microwave oven to 210°C and follow step 1. Place the milk in a jug and cut the butter into it in flakes. Cook on Full (100%) power for 4–4½ minutes until the milk has reached boiling point and the butter has melted. At this stage tip in the flour and beat until smooth. Beat in the eggs. Follow steps 3 and 4, then combination bake at 210°C on Medium (50%) power for 22–24 minutes until richly brown and well risen.

ABOVE RIGHT: Salt-grilled hamburger
BELOW RIGHT: Toad in the clouds

LAMB CUTLETS IN PASTRY

25 g (1 oz) butter or 1 tablespoon vegetable oil
1 large onion, peeled and finely chopped
100 g (4 oz) mushrooms, cleaned and finely chopped
1 garlic clove, peeled and finely chopped
1 tablespoon chopped fresh parsley
salt
freshly ground black pepper
450 g (1 lb) frozen puff pastry, defrosted
8 best end lamb cutlets, trimmed of fat
1 egg, beaten with pinch of salt (egg wash)

To serve:
redcurrant jelly

Preparation time: about 30 minutes
Cooking time: 35–40 minutes
Oven: 220°C, 425°F, Gas Mark 7
Microwave time: about 20 minutes

It is important to have small, neat cutlets, well trimmed of fat and with a long thin bone protruding. You want best end cutlets prepared in the French style. Crimp the pastry, rather like a three-cornered hat, around the meat and glaze with egg.

1. In the butter or oil sauté the onion until softened. Add the mushrooms and sauté until cooked. Stir in the garlic and cook for a minute. Add the parsley and season.
2. Roll out the pastry very thinly and cut into eight triangles, each one just large enough to wrap around the meat.
3. In the cleaned-out sauté pan, quickly brown both sides of the chops in a little more oil or butter to seal them. Remove and let drain. Season the meat.
4. Pour off any liquid from the onion and mushroom mixture. Put a heaped teaspoon of the mixture into the centre of each pastry triangle. Place a cutlet on the stuffing and pinch the pastry around it, making a firm seal. Trim away any excess pastry and if you are feeling creative make little leaves to stick on top of the parcels. Brush on the egg wash.
5. Place the parcels on a wet baking sheet and cook in the preheated oven for 15-20 minutes, or until the pastry is flaky and golden. Serve with redcurrant jelly.

MICROWAVE
Place the butter in a bowl and cook on Full (100%) power for 3½ minutes, stirring once. Add the mushrooms and garlic, blending well. Cover and cook on Full (100%) power for 2 minutes. Add the parsley and season the mixture. Preheat the combination microwave oven to 230°C. Make the lamb parcels as instructed in steps 2–5, place on a large ovenproof plate or dish and combination bake at 230°C on Medium (50%) power for 14–16 minutes or until the pastry is flakey and golden.

BOEUF MIROTON

50 g (2 oz) butter or beef dripping
750 g (1½ lb) large onions, peeled and finely sliced
1–2 bay leaves
1 tablespoon plain flour
450 ml (¾ pint) beef stock
2 teaspoons red wine vinegar
2 teaspoons French mustard
salt
freshly ground black pepper
about 450 g (1 lb) sliced cooked beef
chopped fresh parsley

Preparation time: about 5 minutes
Cooking time: about 40–45 minutes

ABOVE LEFT: Lamb cutlets in pastry
BELOW LEFT: Boeuf miroton

If you do happen to have boiled some beef, use the beef stock in the sauce for the Boeuf Miroton. Or else you will have to resort to a stock cube. It is important that after adding the beef you do no more than warm it through; otherwise it may well become leathery. Boeuf Miroton is good served with plainly boiled, or baked, potatoes and a green salad.

1. Melt the butter or beef dripping in a heavy bottomed pan and gently cook the sliced onions with the bay leaf or leaves. Stew for at least 15 minutes until the mixture softens and turns gold. The longer you cook it, the better, within reason.
2. Add the flour and stir well. Add the stock and vinegar and blend until you have a cohesive sauce. Cook for another 20 minutes or so.
3. Add the mustard, stir and taste for seasoning.
4. Lay the slices of meat on top of the onion mixture. Cover the pan and cook very gently just until the meat is heated through. Sprinkle with chopped parsley and serve.

SALADS AND VEGETABLES

In the same length of time that it takes to overcook cabbage, these excellent vegetable and salad dishes can be prepared. Broad Beans and Peas are a lovely combination, and one that is rarely used, while Rösti remains a great gift from the Swiss to the world. Fattoush, a Syrian salad with an interesting texture and lively flavour, embodies all of summertime, whatever the weather.

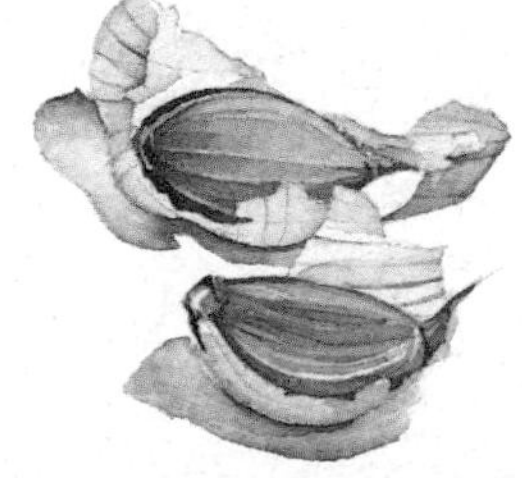

Stir-fried vegetables with curried omelette

PAN BAGNA

SERVES 2–3
1 'slipper' loaf or round flat soft bread or French baguette
150 ml (¼ pint) virgin olive oil
25–50 ml (1–2 fl oz) wine vinegar, to taste
salt
freshly ground black pepper
1 clove of garlic, peeled and crushed
2 large 'Mediterranean' tomatoes
1 large Spanish onion
1 green or red pepper, de-seeded and thinly sliced
1 small tin of anchovy fillets, drained of oil or brine and rinsed
50 g (2 oz) black olives, stoned

Preparation time: 20 minutes, plus 1–2 hours weighting

I am glad to be able to report on a wonderful new group of bread shops with produce so good all you need for a meal would be butter, some ham or cheese and perhaps a bunch of radishes.

The branch of the Italian bakery, La Fornaia, that I visited, is at 66 Notting Hill Gate, London W11. There is another branch in Richmond and one in the Fulham Road. There is an astonishing range of bread and sweet baked goods, including petits fours. I bought an olive bread, studded with green olives and something they called a 'slipper', the description referring to the shape. The texture was slightly chewy, the sweet taste flirting with sour.

The recipe below for Pan Bagna is just one way of using such a bread. A round, flat, soft bread or a French baguette would work equally well.

1. Slice the loaf in half horizontally. Make up a vinaigrette with the oil, wine vinegar to taste, salt, pepper and garlic. Sprinkle the cut sides of the bread liberally with the vinaigrette.
2. Arrange sliced tomatoes, onion and pepper on the bottom half of the bread. Garnish with the anchovy fillets and olives.
3. Place the top half of the bread on the sandwich, wrap it tightly in aluminium foil and leave for an hour or two with weights on top for the flavours to meld and the sandwich to form a solid mass easy to slice and serve.

LENTIL SALAD

SERVES 2
225 g (8 oz) lentils
1 onion, peeled
1 garlic clove
2 bouquet garni or 1 bay leaf
3 tablespoons olive oil
1 tablespoon red wine vinegar
salt
freshly ground black pepper
a pinch of dry mustard
2 hard-boiled eggs, quartered
50 g (2 oz) black olives, stoned
6 anchovies or 4 rashers streaky bacon
1 tablespoon chopped fresh parsley

Preparation time: about 15 minutes
Cooking time: 40–60 minutes
Microwave time: about 23 minutes

Full of iron and the Vitamin B group, lentils are nutritious food and ideal as the basis of a winter-time salad which, when composed as below, can be served as a main course. The small slaty-green lentils, *lentilles de Puy*, are the nicest, and many health-food shops stock them. Lentils need no soaking, but they should be washed and inspected for any little bits of gravel or other undesirable elements. They should take between 40 minutes and an hour to cook, but keep checking because they should not fray at the edges.

1. Wash the lentils as described above. Cover with water, add the peeled onion, the garlic and bouquet garni or bay leaf, and simmer until the lentils are tender. Drain and remove the onion, garlic and bouquet garni or bay leaf.
2. Make a vinaigrette with the olive oil, red wine vinegar, salt and pepper and dry mustard. Toss the warm lentils in the dressing.
3. Garnish with the hard-boiled eggs, the stoned olives and either anchovies or the bacon, first chopped and then fried until crisp. Sprinkle with chopped parsley and serve.

MICROWAVE
If short of time, this dish can be made in the microwave: Place the washed lentils in a dish, cover with boiling water, add the peeled onion, garlic and bouquet garni or bay leaf. Cover and cook on Full (100%) power for 15–20 minutes, stirring once, until tender. Drain and remove the onion, garlic and bouquet garni or bay leaf. Follow steps 2–3. If using bacon, chop and place in a dish. Cook on Full (100%) power for 3 minutes. Drain on absorbent kitchen paper.

LEFT: Pan bagna
FAR LEFT: Lentil salad

CELERIAC AND POTATO PURÉE

1 celeriac, weighing 450 g (1 lb) or more (buy a firm one that is as ungnarled as possible)
225 g (½ lb) potatoes, weighed after peeling
3 fat cloves garlic, peeled (optional)
3 tablespoons cream
50 g (2 oz) butter
salt
generous amounts of freshly ground black pepper

Preparation time: about 5 minutes
Cooking time: about 15 minutes

The root vegetable celeriac seems underrated in this country. Perhaps its appearance, like that of a knobbly alien plant that has fallen to earth, deters people from approaching it and relishing its subtle flavour. It is much used in German cooking and in France nearly every *charcuterie* will have a salad of grated blanched celeriac mixed with a mustardy mayonnaise known as rémoulade. Celeriac makes a good basis for a soup (try mixing in some soaked, dried mushrooms such as porcini) but, to my mind, it is best of all cooked with about half its weight in potatoes and then mashed. Enriched with butter and cream and nudged by the flavour of garlic, the resulting purée can accompany simply grilled meat, poultry or sausages and turn them into an estimable meal.

1. Peel the celeriac which, if it is a knobbly one, takes a bit of energy. Cut it into chunks and drop them immediately into water to stop them browning.
2. Cut the peeled potatoes into pieces of a similar size.
3. In a large pan of salted water, simmer the celeriac, potatoes and peeled garlic cloves until the vegetables are tender. Drain.
4. Mash carefully or, if you have a vegetable mill, turn them through the medium blade.
5. Beat in the cream and butter, and season with salt and pepper.
6. Beat again thoroughly to obtain a smooth mixture and serve as an accompaniment to any simply cooked meat. This can successfully be kept warm in a double boiler.

FENNEL FRITTERS

SERVES 4–6
3–4 fennel bulbs
100 g (4 oz) plain flour
1 teaspoon baking powder
1 egg
1 tablespoon olive oil
150 ml (¼ pint) tepid water
salt
freshly ground black pepper

To serve:
lemon quarters (optional)

Preparation time: 15 minutes
Cooking time: about 10 minutes

I like this Italian notion of making fennel into fritters. They make an interesting and quite luxurious accompaniment to plainly grilled fish or meat or poultry.

1. Trim the fennel bulbs, cut them in half and then in thin segments, each piece held together at the base.
2. Put the flour and baking powder in a bowl. Make a well.
3. Add the egg and olive oil and start to beat.
4. Slowly incorporate the tepid water, then season with salt and pepper.
5. Dip the fennel pieces in the batter and deep-fry in hot oil, preferably olive oil, until brown and crisp.
6. Drain on kitchen paper. These fritters are good served with lemon quarters.

FAR LEFT: Celeriac and potato purée
LEFT: Fennel fritters

STACKED SPINACH PANCAKES

450 g (1 lb) tomatoes
25 g (1 oz) olive oil
2 cloves garlic, peeled and chopped
pinch of sugar
salt
freshly ground black pepper

Filling:
100 g (4 oz) thinly sliced cooked ham
50 g (2 oz) grated Cheddar cheese

Batter:
225 g (8 oz) raw spinach
100 g (4 oz) plain flour
pinch of salt
1 egg
300 ml (½ pint) skimmed milk
1 dessertspoon vegetable oil

Preparation time: about 15 minutes
Cooking time: about 30 minutes
Oven: 200°C, 400°F, Gas Mark 6

I am sure some people are discouraged from cooking by the myths that surround the activity; for example, that pancake batter must be left to stand before it can be cooked. Running late with the children's supper one evening, I made pancakes without letting the batter sit for even a minute and the pancakes were fine – perhaps not the best ever, but absolutely fine. Those described below look prettiest if stacked into a layer cake with your choice of filling or sauce. I have suggested ham, tomato sauce and cheese, but equally you could make an excellent vegetarian supper with fillings such as mushrooms in cream, perhaps, or a purée of sweetcorn alternating with tomato sauce.

1. Cook the spinach, chop to a fine purée and drain thoroughly.
2. To make the pancake batter: sift the flour and salt into a basin. Make a well and drop in the egg. Start to mix with a wooden spoon, slowly incorporating the flour and gradually adding the skimmed milk until you have a smooth batter the consistency of double cream.
3. Mix in the puréed spinach and the vegetable oil. Let sit if you have the chance.
4. During that time make a thick tomato sauce by heating the peeled chopped tomatoes in olive oil, adding the garlic and seasonings and simmering to reduce.
5. Make the pancakes in the usual manner, aiming for six to eight. Keep them warm.
6. In a suitable ovenproof dish layer the pancakes in one stack, like a layer cake, alternating the sliced ham and the tomato sauce as fillings and finishing with the cheese on top.
7. Heat through in a hot oven until the cheese has melted and is golden. Serve cut into wedges.

BROAD BEANS AND PEAS

SERVES 2–4
1 tablespoon vegetable oil
25 g (1 oz) butter
1 bunch of spring onions, cleaned and chopped
450 g (1 lb) fresh broad beans, podded
450 g (1 lb) fresh peas, podded
chicken stock, to cover
1 round lettuce, trimmed and shredded
salt
pinch of sugar
freshly ground black pepper
1 teaspoon chopped fresh dill
2 tablespoons cream (optional)
1 teaspoon cornflour or potato flour (optional)

Preparation time: about 5 minutes
Cooking time: 20–25 minutes

I remember once making several dishes along the lines of the one described below in a seaside village in Greece.

If you cannot find fresh dill, substitute parsley. I like the slithery texture of cooked lettuce but if you don't, you can leave it out and perhaps thicken the juices with a little cream or stock mixed with a teaspoon of cornflour or potato flour. I have made a successful version of this using frozen peas.

1. Heat the oil and butter in a heavy-bottomed pan. Cook the spring onions gently for a few minutes, then add the broad beans and cook for a few minutes. If the broad beans are tiny, they can be cooked with the peas.
2. Add the peas and turn them to glaze with the buttery oil.
3. Add enough stock to come just level with the vegetables, then the lettuce, a pinch of salt and sugar and the black pepper.
4. Cover and simmer gently until the vegetables are tender – about 10–15 minutes. Check there is no scorching, but there should be no need for additional liquid.
5. Add the dill and cream, if using.
6. If you want a thicker sauce, mix 1 teaspoon cornflour or potato flour in a little more stock. Add and shake the pan to blend.

ABOVE RIGHT: Stacked spinach pancakes
BELOW RIGHT: Broad beans and peas

HOT RUNNER BEAN AND BACON SALAD

1 kg (2 lb) runner beans
10 rashers of streaky bacon
2 tablespoons vegetable oil
3 tablespoons soft fresh breadcrumbs
2 tablespoons red wine vinegar
salt
freshly ground black pepper

Preparation time: 30 minutes
Cooking time: about 25 minutes

1. Trim the beans at the ends and if there is any suspicion of strings, run your knife down each edge, cutting away a fine strip. Slice them on the diagonal. Put to cook in plenty of salted boiling water until just tender and drain.
2. Chop the bacon finely and fry gently until crisp, add the oil and the breadcrumbs and fry until the crumbs are golden and crunchy.
3. Pile the beans into a hot dish. Scatter the bacon and crumbs over the beans.
4. Now, into the hot pan where you have been frying the bacon, pour the wine vinegar. Let it bubble and frazzle and when it is reduced to about 1 tablespoon, dribble it over the beans. Season.

ASPARAGUS WITH RED PEPPER PURÉE

450 g (1 lb) asparagus
2 sweet red peppers
1 clove of garlic, peeled and chopped
1–2 anchovies, drained of olive oil or brine and rinsed (optional)
salt
freshly ground black pepper
pinch of sugar

Preparation time: 10 minutes
Cooking time: about 30 minutes

As a change from the usual vinaigrette, Hollandaise and beurre blanc, this very modern red pepper purée might appeal.

1. Trim the asparagus and cook, tied into bundles, in boiling salted water, testing after 10 minutes as you want them tender but not waterlogged. Drain on a tea-towel.
2. Char the red peppers under the grill, put them in a polythene bag for 5 minutes to steam and then peel off the skin. This removes the possibility of bitterness and adds a smoky flavour.
3. Remove all seeds and pith, chop into squares and boil with the garlic in enough of the asparagus water to cover, until tender. Alternatively, you can just trim and de-seed the peppers, cut up and cook.
4. When they are tender, liquidize with a little of the cooking liquid and the anchovies, if using them. Season with salt, pepper and sugar and serve immediately.

CHICKPEAS WITH SPINACH

2 medium onions
olive oil, as required
500 g (1 lb 4 oz) frozen leaf spinach
400 g (2×14 oz) cans chickpeas
1 dried red chilli, crumbled
salt
freshly ground black pepper
2 slices white or brown bread
1 large garlic clove, finely chopped

Preparation time: about 10 minutes
Cooking time: about 20 minutes

TOP LEFT: Hot runner bean and bacon salad
LEFT: Asparagus with red pepper purèe
BOTTOM LEFT: Chickpeas with spinach

An item that emerges from a tin fairly unscathed is chickpeas. I dare say their quality of seemingly never becoming overcooked, even when you soak dried ones and boil them for hours, is a contributory factor. You can make instant hummus with tinned chickpeas whizzed in a food processor with olive oil, lemon juice, and tahini (sesame paste) – better and cheaper than the little pots of the stuff. Or you can try the recipe below, which has ingredients you can buy at the last minute.

1. Peel the onions and slice from tip to base in thin crescents. Fry them until golden in 1 tablespoon olive oil.
2. Add the leaf spinach and cook according to the packet instructions until softened. Drain away any excess water.
3. Drain the chickpeas and stir into the spinach with a dribble more of olive oil and the crumbled chilli pepper. Cover the pan and allow to simmer. Season.
4. Meanwhile, fry the bread in olive oil with the finely chopped garlic. When the bread is golden, drain on kitchen paper and then crumble it roughly on to the spinach and chickpeas.
5. You could, if you wish, fry another slice of bread, cut it into triangles and tuck into the corners of the finished dish. Eat before the crumbs have lost their crunch.

CAULIFLOWER WITH MUSTARD SEEDS

1 large cauliflower
2 tablespoons vegetable oil or butter, or a mixture of the two
2 teaspoons yellow or black mustard seeds
2.5 cm (1 inch) cube fresh ginger root, peeled and finely slivered, or ½ teaspoon powdered ginger
2 fat garlic cloves, peeled and finely chopped
2 teaspoons cumin seeds or fennel seeds
½ teaspoon paprika
freshly ground black pepper
salt
about 1 tablespoon water

Preparation time: 5–10 minutes
Cooking time: about 20 minutes

Cauliflower needs a bit of kick and crunch, which can be provided by dressing it with a vinaigrette whilst it is still warm, then scattering chopped bacon and fried breadcrumbs and parsley on top, or by following this recipe. It is quick to make and rather healthy and stands up perfectly well to being a course on its own.

1. Trim the cauliflower of any dodgy bits. Remove the green leaves and the large stalks, and break the cauliflower up into really quite small florets. You want to end up with some pieces almost the size of large crumbs.
2. Heat the butter or oil (or make a mixture of the two; the butter is really there for the flavour) and add the mustard seeds. When they begin to pop add the ginger (powdered ginger should be added with the cauliflower) and fry briefly. Add the garlic and stir around, but don't let it catch.
3. Add the cauliflower pieces, stir-fry, and then include the cumin or fennel seeds, paprika, and a good few turns of the pepper mill. Keep stirring, season with salt and sprinkle on about a tablespoon of water.
4. Cover the pan and turn the heat up high for 1 minute to build up steam. Turn the heat low and cook for about 3 minutes. Test for tenderness.
5. Cook off any remaining moisture with the lid of the pan removed. Stir and serve. The cauliflower should be slightly crisp.

FATTOUSH

1 small cucumber, peeled and chopped into cubes
salt
1 normal or 2 small pittas
6 tablespoons lemon juice
3 firm tomatoes, skinned, chopped and seeded
heart of a Cos lettuce, shredded
1 bunch spring onions, cleaned and finely chopped
2 tablespoons chopped fresh mint or 1 tablespoon dried mint
2 tablespoons chopped fresh parsley
2 tablespoons chopped purslane leaves (optional)
1 tablespoon chopped coriander leaves (optional)
2 garlic cloves, peeled and crushed
6–8 tablespoons olive oil
freshly ground black pepper

Preparation time: about 40 minutes
Cooking time: about 5 minutes

Fattoush is one of my favourite summer salads. It is a Syrian peasant dish, a salad with an interesting texture and lively flavour, very much appreciated all over the Middle East. It can be served as a first course, a light lunch, or as part of a meze. It might occur to you that it is a way of using leftover pitta. If that is your plan, do not omit the warming process before incorporating it in the salad. Purslane, sometimes known as continental watercress, is sometimes available in Greek or Cypriot grocers and is an optional, but enhancing, ingredient. Try to find the flat-leafed variety of parsley.

1. Before beginning the salad, put the cubed cucumber into a colander, sprinkle with salt and leave to drain for about half an hour. If you miss out this step you risk making the salad soggy.
2. Heat the pitta bread under the grill until hot but not stiff. Pull into small pieces and put into a salad bowl. Pour on the lemon juice and let the bread mop it up. If you want a less domineering lemon flavour, use half the amount of juice plus 1 tablespoon water.
3. Rinse the salt from the cucumber, pat it dry and place it plus the other ingredients in the salad bowl. Toss very thoroughly. Taste for seasoning, adjusting amounts of lemon juice, oil, salt and pepper to taste.

ABOVE RIGHT: Cauliflower with mustard seeds
BELOW RIGHT: Fattoush

RÖSTI

SERVES 3-4
750 g–1 kg (1½–2 lb) large potatoes, peeled and cooked
25 g (1 oz) butter
1 tablespoon olive oil or other vegetable oil
salt
freshly ground black pepper

Preparation time: about 10 minutes
Cooking time: about 30 minutes

The reason that Swiss, or Swiss-trained, hoteliers are the best in the world is because the Swiss do everything correctly. Unimaginatively maybe, but correctly. It is important to make this dish correctly and put to the back of your non-Swiss mind ideas like throwing in some chopped ham or a handful of peas. Parboiled or steamed potatoes, butter and oil are all you need along with, preferably, a heavy non-stick frying pan. If plain grated potatoes sounds just too dull for words, you could, I suppose, mix in some grated Emmental cheese, but try it simply first. It makes a superb accompaniment to roast game.

1. The counsel of perfection is to peel then parboil the potatoes for 7 minutes, drain them and let them cool overnight in the refrigerator. This makes a difference to their texture, which, in turn, makes a difference to the finished dish, but if it's not possible just try to cook them somewhat ahead of time. Grate the potatoes using a coarse grater.
2. Warm the butter and oil in a 23 cm (9 inch) diameter heavy non-stick frying pan, or one more or less that size. Spread the grated potato evenly in the pan, and sprinkle with salt and pepper. Put a plate of appropriate size upside down over the potatoes; the plate should fit in the pan, not sit on top of it. Cook gently for 15-20 minutes, until cooked through.
3. Turn the rösti out of the pan by putting a wooden board, or similar, over plate and pan and turning the whole thing over. You should now have a circular potato cake sitting on the plate, ready to be cut into slices.

SEAWEED

2 heads of bouncy looking spring greens, or you could use kale
vegetable oil, for deep-frying
pinch of caster sugar
1 tablespoon desiccated coconut (optional)
1 tablespoon chopped dried prawns, available in oriental supermarkets (optional) or crabmeat (optional)

Preparation time: 15 minutes
Cooking time: 10 minutes

ABOVE LEFT: Rösti
BELOW LEFT: Seaweed

After you have tried this recipe you will not pay the almost invariably excessive prices asked for 'seaweed' as a first course on a Chinese restaurant menu. It is not a kind of algae, but good old spring greens sliced into threads and deep-fried in oil until they crackle like cellophane. When eating at home, use it as a vegetable rather than serving it as a first course, since it could look rather lonely on the plate. It is excellent with simply cooked fish. People who crouch in cupboards at the sound of the word 'greens' will be won over by this way of treating them.

1. Trim away any discoloured leaves from the greens and, taking a few leaves at a time, roll them up into neat cylinders to facilitate making thin strips. Using a very sharp knife, cut across the cylinders in fine slices.
2. Heat enough vegetable oil to deep-fry batches of your heap of threads. When it is nearly smoking hot drop in handfuls of the greens, avoiding crowding the pot, and cook briefly until they are translucent and crackly.
3. Remove and drain on kitchen paper and, while very hot, sprinkle with just a pinch of caster sugar. It adds an intriguing crunch and sweetness.
4. If you want to garnish the 'seaweed' you could toast some desiccated coconut until golden in a dry iron pan or finely chop some dried prawns, which would faintly resemble the shredded dried scallop used in Chinese restaurants. It occurs to me that crabmeat, preferably fresh, but defrosted or out of a tin, if that sounds more plausible, would be a good accompaniment.

AUTHENTIC CAESAR SALAD

1 large Cos lettuce or 2 smaller ones
2 eggs
3 slices good white bread
2 fat garlic cloves
6 tablespoons olive oil
sea salt
freshly ground black pepper
juice of½ lemon
150 g (2 oz) can anchovies, drained and rinsed
50 g (2 oz) Parmesan cheese, freshly grated

Preparation time: about 30 minutes
Cooking time: about 12 minutes

1. Wash the lettuce and dry thoroughly.
2. Near to the time of serving, assemble all the other ingredients and set the water to boil for the eggs. Trim the crusts from the bread and cut it into cubes.
3. Crush the garlic into half the olive oil and fry the bread croûtons in this.
4. Place the lettuce in a large salad bowl and add 2 tablespoons olive oil. Sprinkle on some sea salt and freshly ground pepper. Toss with another tablespoon of olive oil.
5. Pour on the lemon juice, the drained and chopped anchovies and break in the yolks of the eggs that you have plunged into boiling water for 1 minute. Toss once.
6. Sprinkle on the Parmesan. Toss again and add the croûtons. Serve immediately.

TIAN

450 g (1 lb) courgettes, trimmed and grated
salt
350 g (12 oz) fresh spinach, washed
1 large onion, peeled and chopped
3 tablespoons good olive oil
3 garlic cloves, peeled and slivered
50 g (2 oz) cooked rice
freshly ground black pepper
3 eggs
75 g (3 oz) hard cheese, grated (Cheddar Gruyère, Parmesan or a mixture)
50 g (2 oz) fresh breadcrumbs

Preparation time: about 25 minutes
Cooking time: about 45 minutes
Oven: 180°C, 350°F, Gas Mark 4

1. Put the grated courgettes in a sieve, salt them lightly and leave to 'perspire'.
2. Cook the spinach in boiling salted water until limp. Refresh in cold water, drain well and chop finely.
3. Wring the salted courgettes in a clean tea-towel to extract their moisture.
4. Sauté the chopped onion in the olive oil and, when it starts to brown, add the garlic. Stir round. Add the courgettes and cook for a few minutes, then stir in the spinach and cook for a few minutes more. Stir in the rice and season.
5. Beat the eggs in a large bowl, then stir in the vegetable mixture.
6. Oil a shallow gratin dish (earthenware is traditional), and spread the mixture in it. Mix together the grated cheese and breadcrumbs and sprinkle over the top. Bake for about 35 minutes in the preheated oven.

CORN FRITTERS

4 cobs fresh sweetcorn
2 eggs
65 ml (2½ fl oz) milk
½ tablespoon melted butter
3 tablespoons plain flour
½ teaspoon baking powder
salt
freshly ground black pepper
sunflower oil or other vegetable oil, as required

Preparation time: about 30 minutes
Cooking time: about 15 minutes

1. Clean the cobs of leaves and strands of 'silk' and, holding the cobs vertical, slice off the kernels with a sharp knife. Put into a bowl and, with the back of the knife, scrape the cobs to release the milky juices.
2. Beat together the eggs, milk and melted butter.
3. Into another bowl, sift the flour, baking powder and a pinch of salt. Using a wooden spoon, make a well in the flour and slowly beat the egg mixture into the flour until you achieve a smooth batter.
4. Tip in the prepared corn and mix. Season with freshly ground black pepper.
5. Pour a thin film of oil into a frying pan, heat and drop tablespoons of the batter on to it, each an inch or so apart. Flatten them slightly, if necessary, and cook until golden brown. Turn and cook the other side.
6. Drain quickly on kitchen paper and serve with meat, bacon or grilled fish.

LEFT: Authentic Caesar salad
FAR LEFT: Tiân
BELOW LEFT: Corn fritters

STIR-FRIED VEGETABLES WITH CURRIED OMELETTE

SERVES 2
vegetable oil
50 g (2 oz) shallots or spring onions, peeled and sliced
1 large carrot, peeled and thinly sliced
100 g (4 oz) mangetout peas, trimmed
50 g (2 oz) thin green beans, chopped into 2.5 cm (1 inch) lengths
2 courgettes, cut into matchsticks or thin ribbons with a vegetable peeler
100 g (4 oz) broccoli florets
1 fat garlic clove, peeled and cut into slivers
salt
2 eggs
2 teaspoons water
freshly ground black pepper
2 teaspoons curry powder or garam masala

Preparation time: about 15 minutes
Cooking time: about 20 minutes

Any mixture of vegetables can be stir-fried, but sometimes the simpler the combination the better. This dish, which I quite often make when I'm in for supper by myself, works perfectly well just with onions and carrots, but if you want a lighter, greener look, try an assembly along the lines of mangetouts, broccoli florets, spring onions and courgettes. When making the curried omelettes, do one at a time to keep the oil hot enough to puff them up dramatically. Otherwise they droop rather discouragingly. The notion of omelette as a garnish can be extended to other dishes. Strips of omelette, for example, are good in consommé. I have given a guideline to a choice of vegetables; use your imagination but not, I think, the cabbage family.

1. Here is the moment your wok, should you have one, can come into its own. In that, or a frying pan, heat about 1 tablespoon of vegetable oil. Add the prepared shallots or spring onions, carrot, mangetouts and beans and stir-fry.
2. A few minutes later, add the courgettes, broccoli and garlic, and stir-fry for a few more minutes, until the vegetables are hot and cooked but still crunchy. Sprinkle with salt. Keep warm on a low heat while you make the omelettes.
3. Beat 1 egg with 1 teaspoon water in a bowl. Season lightly with salt and pepper.
4. In a small frying pan make extremely hot 1 dessertspoon vegetable oil. Quickly add 1 teaspoon curry powder or garam masala to remove the raw taste, and pour in the egg. It should puff up. When it does, flip it over and it will rise to even greater heights.
5. Serve the omelette immediately on top of the vegetables and, halfway through the meal, make another omelette the same way.

COLCANNON

1 kg (2 lb) potatoes (a large floury variety), peeled and cooked
1 small cabbage or 450 g (1 lb) kale, which is traditional
150-300 ml (¼–½ pint) creamy milk
salt
freshly ground black pepper
100 g (4 oz) butter, melted

Preparation time: about 15 minutes
Cooking time: about 30 minutes

ABOVE LEFT: Stir-fried vegetables with curried omelette
BELOW LEFT: Colcannon

I think potatoes are very underrated, or, perhaps more accurately, under-used. They are not inherently fattening – it is the chip fat or butter lavished on them that loads them with calories – and they can be made so delicious that meat is hardly necessary.

1. My tip for mashed potatoes is to boil them mercilessly until they are waterlogged and falling apart and then not to drain them too carefully so that they remain wet which, surprisingly, ultimately makes them lighter.
2. Tidy up, core and finely chop the cabbage or kale. Put it into a small quantity of boiling water and cook quickly, turning it occasionally until it is done.
3. Mash the cooked drained potatoes. Heat the milk and beat enough of it into the potatoes to give a soft, but not sloppy consistency. Stir in the cabbage. Season to taste.
4. Ensuring that the mixture is as hot as possible, pile it into a shallow dish. Make a well large enough to hold the melted butter in the centre and pour it in. If you serve the colcannon straight on to four heated plates, adding a quarter of the butter to each plate, you can eat it by taking forkfuls and dipping them into the butter, which is part of the joy of the dish.

PUDDINGS AND DESSERTS

Just because you are short of time doesn't mean that you and your guests have to forego a treat at the end of the meal. Only those with iron resolution will be able to resist these delectable desserts. More healthy-minded people may want to stick to the fruitier ones, such as Plum Crusts or Fruit Fritters, but for a real indulgence, the Treacle Tart or Creme Brûlée are musts.

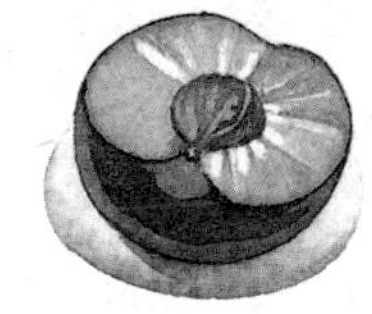

Pecan pie

PROPER CUSTARD

MAKES 600 ml (1 pint)
6 egg yolks
75–100 g (3-4 oz) caster sugar
¼ teaspoon salt
600 ml (1 pint) creamy milk or single cream
1 vanilla pod

Preparation time: about 5 minutes
Cooking time: 15–20 minutes

La crème anglaise is a name the French give to custard. It brings to mind something a little more silky and seductive than the bright yellow sauce of school days, made with a powder and destined to form a geriatric skin. A proper English custard is a thing of pride. Using only egg yolks, sugar, a vanilla pod and creamy milk or single cream, a custard is easy to make and will add finesse to certain puddings, for example, some of the good bottled fruits now available. Once cooled and set, the custard can be coated with an even layer of sugar and then grilled under fierce heat, which will result in crème brûlée. Poached meringues perched on top produces floating islands. By caramelizing sugar, pouring it into the base of the dish and baking the custard you make crème caramel. You needn't use flour or even the tiniest pinch of cornflour. The yolks themselves provide the emulsion.

1. In the top pan of a double boiler, combine the egg yolks, sugar and salt. Set aside.
2. In the bottom saucepan heat the milk or cream with the vanilla pod until it steams but does not boil. Strain the liquid on to the yolks, stirring.
3. Now fill the bottom pan with hot water and cook the custard over simmering water, stirring constantly until the mixture coats the back of a metal spoon.
4. Use as a sauce, or cool and chill in a shallow dish until set.

TARTE TATIN

SERVES 4–6
6-7 dessert apples, cored and quartered
3 tablespoons lemon juice
100 g (4 oz) butter
175 g (6 oz) sugar (brown or white)
a pinch of cinnamon
225 g (8 oz) bought or home-made pastry of your choice

Preparation time: about 30 minutes
Cooking time: 35 minutes
Oven: 200°C, 400°F Gas Mark 6 (or hotter if using puff pastry: follow packet instructions)

Evidently the two spinster sisters Tatin were an impoverished pair and cooked this tart, a favourite of their father's, to earn a living. The point about it is that the pastry is cooked on top, which keeps it light and crisp, while the apples caramelize beneath. To serve, you can turn it out of its pan and hand round with it either whipped cream, crème fraîche or thick Greek yogurt.

The choice of pastry can be a matter of preference – either puff pastry, a sweetened shortcrust, or pâte sablée, which is basically a shortbread mixture. It is important to have a round pan, which you can first heat on the stove and later transfer to the oven. An enamelled iron pan would be ideal. The recipe is traditionally made with apples, but pears work too.

1. Sprinkle the apples with lemon juice to prevent them browning.
2. Spread the butter over the base of your pan and then sprinkle on the sugar, mixed with the pinch of cinnamon, in an even layer. Arrange the apples on top.
3. Roll out your choice of pastry, having given it a chance to rest for 20 minutes or so if it is home-made. Lay the pastry over the apples and trim off any excess, leaving a generous border.
4. Set the pan over fairly high heat on top of the stove and cook until the butter and sugar have bubbled for about 5 minutes. You can peek under the pastry to check, but the smell should tell you when this is happening and if it is starting to burn.
5. Now bake in the preheated oven for 20 minutes or until the pastry is golden. When it is cooked, remove and carefully invert the tart on to a large round serving dish. Eat hot or warm, but not cold.

ABOVE RIGHT: Proper custard
BELOW RIGHT: Tarte tatin

ECONOMICAL CUSTARD

MAKES 300 ml (½ pint)
300 ml (½ pint) milk
1 tablespoon sugar
2 egg yolks
a few drops of vanilla essence

Preparation time: about 5 minutes
Cooking time: 15–20 minutes

This is a more economical and less heart-rending recipe that you can use in the same way as that on page 106.

1. Heat the milk and sugar and bring slowly to the boil.
2. Beat the yolks in a bowl.
3. Pour the milk on to the yolks, stirring steadily.
4. Return to the pan and stir over gentle heat until thickened. Add the vanilla essence.

GUILT-FREE TREACLE TART

SERVES 4–6
225 g (8 oz) plain flour
a pinch of salt
100 g (4 oz) butter or margerine
50 g (2 oz) lard
1 egg yolk
juice and grated rind of 2 lemons
5 tablespoons golden syrup
100 g (4 oz) fresh brown breadcrumbs
1 thin-skinned orange, washed but not peeled, and thinly sliced

Preparation time: about 35 minutes, plus resting
Cooking time: 25–30 minutes
Oven: 200°C, 400°F, Gas Mark 6
Microwave time: 20 minutes

ABOVE LEFT: Economical custard
BELOW LEFT: Guilt-free treacle tart

By almost no stretch of the imagination could you think of treacle tart as being beneficial to your system, but it is one of those simple and simply delicious desserts that should not be brushed aside in the current upsurge of culinary moral fervour. By using *brown* breadcrumbs, incorporating the *zest* of lemons and dwelling on the Vitamin C content of oranges you can almost convince yourself that treacle tart is germane to fitness. To make matters worse, enjoy this with whipped cream.

1. Sift the flour into a mixing bowl and sprinkle on the salt. Cut in the fats with a knife and then work the mixture with your fingertips until you arrive at the consistency of uneven breadcrumbs.
2. Using the knife again, mix in the egg yolk, and juice and rind of 1 lemon. To get a cohesive mixture you may need a little cold water. Gather into a ball and, if possible, leave in the fridge for an hour.
3. Roll out the pastry on a floured board. Line a 20 cm (8 inch) pie tin and prick the base of the pastry.
4. Mix together the syrup, breadcrumbs and juice and rind of the other lemon. Pour into the pastry case.
5. Arrange the orange slices, overlapping, on the surface. Bake for 25–30 minutes. Serve lukewarm.

MICROWAVE
If short of time, this dish can be cooked in the microwave: Preheat the combination microwave oven to 200°C. Follow steps 1–4, then arrange the orange slices, overlapping, on the surface. Combination bake at 200°C on Low (30%) power for 20 minutes. Serve lukewarm.

PECAN PIE

about 225 g (8 oz) bought or home-made shortcrust pastry to line a 23 cm (9 inch) pie dish
3 eggs
65 g (2½ oz) butter, melted
150 g (5 oz) sugar
½ teaspoon salt
175 g (6 oz) corn syrup or pouring golden syrup
150 g (5 oz) shelled and halved pecan nuts

Preparation time: about 15 minutes, plus resting
Cooking time: 35 minutes
Oven: 190°C, 375°F, Gas Mark 5
Microwave time: 17 minutes

That Americans are particularly hot on baking is not always apparent in American restaurants here, where the cheesecakes, chocolate cakes, apple pies and pecan pies often taste as if they are all delivered from a rather poor central source of supply. This recipe, which comes from an American living in Britain, is delightfully simple and also delicious. Try to buy pecans in their shells and shell them yourself as the ready-to-use kind sold in plastic containers often seem to have a mustiness about them. Corn syrup is usually used for pecan pie, but a good substitute is the golden syrup that is now sold in bottles for pouring.

1. Roll out the pastry, let it rest for 15 minutes and then line the pie dish.
2. Beat together the eggs, butter, sugar, salt and syrup. Stir in the pecan halves.
3. Pour into the pastry case. Bake for about 35 minutes or until the filling is set and the pastry golden brown.

MICROWAVE
If short of time, this dish can be cooked in the microwave: Preheat the combination microwave oven to 200°C. Follow steps 1 and 2, then pour into the pastry case. Combination bake at 200°C on Low (30%) power for 15 minutes then on 200°C on Full (100%) power for 2 minutes until the filling is set and the pastry is golden brown. (If the top of the pie shows signs of becoming too brown during cooking, then reduce the oven temperature to 180°C.)

PLUM CRUSTS

75 g (3 oz) butter
4 thick slices crusty new white bread, cut from a loaf
1 kg (2 lb) ripe plums
100 g (4 oz) brown sugar
thick cream to serve

Preparation time: about 15 minutes
Cooking time: at least 30 minutes
Oven: 180°C, 350°F, Gas Mark 4

Plums in season beckon you to make jam and chutney; so satisfying to look at the gleaming jars with carefully written labels, so handy to give away as presents. But should your mood not be helping-hands-at-home, here is something more immediate to do with plums.

1. Butter the slices of bread on both sides.
2. Halve the plums and winkle out the stones.
3. Press plums with cavities upwards neatly on to the slices of bread. Into each hollow put a dab of butter and a teaspoon of brown sugar.
4. Place the bread in a baking dish, cover with foil or buttered paper and cook near the top of the oven for 30 minutes. The bread should be golden and crispy, the fruit syrupy. If not, remove foil or paper and cook a little longer.
5. Serve hot with cold, thick cream.

RIGHT: Pecan pie
FAR RIGHT: Plum crusts

BLACKBERRY AND APPLE CRUMBLE

SERVES 4–6
450 g (1 lb) cooking apples, peeled, cored and chopped
50–100 g (2–4 oz) sugar, to taste
5 cm (2 inch) strip of lemon peel
450 g (1 lb) blackberries
100 g (4 oz) flour, or 75 g (3 oz) flour and 2 tablespoons muesli
100 g (4 oz) demerara sugar
50 g (2 oz) ground almonds
100 g (4 oz) butter

Preparation time: about 15 minutes
Cooking time: 40–50 minutes
Oven: 180°C, 350°F, Gas Mark 4
Microwave time: about 24 minutes

A crumble always strikes me as preferable to a pie because of the texture.

1. Put the apples in a saucepan with a splash of water and cook gently with a little sugar and the lemon peel.
2. When the apples are softened, add the blackberries and simmer very gently until they are heated through.
3. Put into a pie dish, keeping back any excess of juice.
4. Rub together the crumble ingredients until you have a mixture with the texture of breadcrumbs. Muesli is good to add.
5. Sprinkle over the fruit and bake in a hot oven until the crumble is browned and crisp. If serving with double cream, add some reserved juice as you beat the cream, to slightly flavour and colour it.

MICROWAVE
Place the apples in a bowl with the sugar and lemon peel. Add a little water, cover and cook on Full (100%) power for 4 minutes until softened. Add the blackberries. Spoon into a pie dish, keeping back any excess of juice. Preheat a combination microwave oven (if using) to 200°C. Follow steps 4 and 5, but combination bake at 200°C on Low (30%) power for 15–20 minutes or cook by microwave only on Full (100%) power for 14–16 minutes then brown under a preheated hot grill until golden.

FRUIT FRITTERS

SERVES ANY NUMBER
fruit of choice
2 tablespoons lemon juice
caster sugar, for sprinkling
vegetable oil, for deep-frying

Batter 1
100 g (4 oz) plain flour, with a pinch of salt
2 tablespoons vegetable oil
150 ml (¼ pint) tepid water
1 egg white

Batter 2:
90 g (3½ oz) flour, with a pinch of salt
1 egg, separated
5 tablespoons tepid beer
about 2 tablespoons water
25 g (1 oz) butter, melted
1 tablespoon Cognac or similar

Preparation time: about 15 minutes
Cooking time: about 10–15 minutes

I remember as a child always being extremely pleased when my mother made apple or banana fritters for pudding, but I realize that I have never done that for my children. Perhaps the current obsession with healthy eating is causing us to forget agreeable old-fashioned ideas. You can usually assemble fritters from what is available in the house, which makes them a good spur-of-the moment idea for a dessert. I have given two recipes for batter below, one rather more ambitious than the other, both lighter than an ordinary pancake batter.

1. For batter 1, sift the flour and salt into a bowl. Add the oil and then the water, beating it in with a wire whisk and keeping going until you have a smooth mixture. Let sit for about an hour, then, just before using, whisk the egg white until stiff and fold in.
2. For batter 2, sift the flour into a bowl. Add the egg yolk, beer and water and slowly incorporate the flour into the liquid. Stir in the butter and your choice of alcohol. Let rest and, before frying, beat the egg white stiffly and fold it into the mixture.
3. To make the fritters, cut your choice of fruit into bite-size pieces and sprinkle with a little lemon juice and sugar if it needs it. Go beyond apple and banana; try apricots or plums.
4. Bring vegetable oil for deep-frying to a high temperature, coat the pieces of fruit in batter and fry until golden, turning over once. Drain on kitchen paper. Sprinkle with sugar and serve immediately.

FAR LEFT: Blackberry and apple crumble
BOTTOM LEFT: Fruit fritters

CLAFOUTIS

3 tablespoons plain flour
a pinch of salt
3 tablespoons caster sugar, preferably vanilla sugar (ie stored with a vanilla pod in it)
2 whole eggs
1 egg yolk
1 tablespoon vegetable oil
300 ml (½ pint) milk
450 g (1 lb) dark sweet cherries
icing sugar or caster sugar, to sift over the top

Preparation time: about 30 minutes
Cooking time: 40–45 minutes
Oven: 180°C, 350°F, Gas Mark 4
Microwave time: 14-15 minutes

'Can she bake a cherry pie?' has always struck me as a rather odd qualification for marriage, if indeed it was marriage that was sought after by Billy Boy. But it is probably as good as any and better than some. Clafoutis is not exactly a pie, though the texture of the batter after cooking should be such that it can be sliced. It is one of the best ways of using cherries if you want to go a step further than eating them raw. A cherry stoner is quite a useful gadget to possess – it can also be used on olives.

1. Sift the flour with a pinch of salt and the sugar into a mixing bowl. Make a well in the centre and add the eggs and egg yolk. Work in the flour slowly with a wooden spoon, as if making pancake batter, which is more or less what you are doing. When smooth, beat in the oil. Gradually beat in the milk until you have a thin batter.
2. Set aside while you stone the cherries, doing this over a bowl to save the drips of juice.
3. Butter an ovenproof dish of about 25 cm (10 inch) diameter or an equivalent oblong size. Put the cherries and their juice on the bottom. Pour on the batter, tipping it over the back of a spoon to avoid jostling the cherries.
4. Bake for 40–45 minutes or until a knife blade slipped in comes out clean.
5. Dust with icing sugar or caster sugar and serve warm. Alternatively, let the clafoutis cool, unmould and cut into wedges.

MICROWAVE

If short of time, this pudding can be made in the microwave: Preheat the combination microwave oven to 250°C. Follow steps 1–3, then combination bake at 250°C on Medium (50%) power for 14–15 minutes or until a knife blade slipped in comes out clean. Dust with icing sugar or caster sugar to serve.

RHUBARB FOOL

1 kg (2 lb) young rhubarb
100–175 g (4–6 oz) demerara sugar, depending on how tart you like your dessert
finely grated rind of 1 small orange
275 ml (9 fl oz) cream or custard
2 teaspoons Pernod (optional but good)
a little preserved ginger in syrup, chopped small (optional decoration)

Preparation time: about 25 minutes
Cooking time: about 5 minutes

Rhubarb fool can be made just of the carefully stewed fruit with perhaps a little orange or ginger as flavouring and thick cream stirred in not too thoroughly so as to achieve a marbled effect. If you wish, you can use custard in place of cream. If so, make the custard with 300 ml (½ pint) single cream and 3 egg yolks. For a less rich dish, stew the fruit as directed and serve with soured cream or thick Greek yogurt sprinkled with a little demerara sugar. The best accompaniment to rhubarb fool is slices of plain sponge cake gently fried in butter. A slightly stale sponge cake is all to the good. Gooseberries are also good to fool, but omit the flavouring of Pernod and substitute elderflower wine or Frontignan.

1. Trim the rhubarb stalks of any leaves or brown roots. Chop into 5 cm (2 inch) lengths. Put into a heavy saucepan or ovenproof dish with the sugar, just a little water and the orange rind. Simmer or cook in a low oven for about 5 minutes, or until the fruit is tender.
2. Drain off excess juice. Either sieve, blend or leave the fruit whole – the last would be my choice.
3. When cold, stir in the cream or custard (see page 106 or 109) and the Pernod if you are using it. Serve in a china or pottery bowl rather than a glass one. Decorate, if you like, with preserved ginger.

ABOVE RIGHT: Clafoutis
BELOW RIGHT: Rhubarb fool

BAKING

These are recipes which bury the notion that baking is a time-consuming occupation. They are extremely quick mixtures to put together and even their cooking time is not particularly long. The most hastily assembled meal can be lifted into another class by the addition of something home-baked, preferably served warm.

Eggie's biscuits and Brandy snaps

BROWN SODA BREAD

275 g (10 oz) wholemeal flour
175 g (6 oz) plain white bread flour
3 teaspoons baking powder
1 teaspoon bicarbonate of soda
2 teaspoons salt
300 ml (½ pint) butter milk or milk soured with lemon juice
1 egg, beaten, and another to glaze (optional)

Preparation time: about 15 minutes
Cooking time: 35–40 minutes
Oven: 190°C, 375°F, Gas Mark 5

Despite the dismal fact that *nouvelle cuisine* is now all the go in Ireland – it seems particularly inappropriate there – I noticed when I visited the country that mercifully there was no shortage of the delicious salty Irish brown soda bread. A request for bread summoned up the real thing. The great plus about soda bread is the speed with which it can be made; none of that diddling around waiting for it to prove itself. From start to finish it can be made in less than an hour and it will make any meal, even a shop-bought one, feel wholesome.

1. Sift together the two flours, baking powder, soda and salt. If you are using a coarse brown flour, do not bother sifting it.
2. Mix together the buttermilk or soured milk and the egg and stir them into the dry ingredients.
3. Mix roughly with a spoon or knife and then knead on a floured surface for a few minutes until smooth.
4. Shape into a round, flat cake and put on to a greased baking sheet. Using a knife, make a deep cross on the round and bake in a preheated oven for 35–40 minutes.
5. If you wish to glaze the bread, brush with a beaten egg and return to the oven for a few minutes.

CORNBREAD

65 g (2½ oz) plain flour, sifted
200 g (7 oz) corn meal
1 teaspoon salt
1 teaspoon sugar
2 teaspoons baking powder
2 eggs, well beaten
250 ml (8 fl oz) milk
50 ml (2 fl oz) cream
2½ tablespoons melted butter

Preparation time: about 10 minutes
Cooking time: 15–20 minutes
Oven: 200°C, 400°F, Gas Mark 6

Cornbread, much loved in the Southern states of America, is reasonably quick to prepare and once you agree to accept, as Americans readily do, a sweetish carbohydrate accompaniment to a savoury main course, you and your guests will appreciate the cakey consistency and the Scarlett O'Hara graciousness of warm cornbread served alongside, say, a microwaved frozen chicken fricassee.

The recipe below comes from James Beard's book on American Cookery. He got it from a Mrs Jeanne Owen, 'a stalwart disciple of the art of good living'. I have converted the quantities from those maddening cup measurements the Americans go in for, so use your judgement over consistency. Leftover cornbread mixed with sautéed onions, crumbled fried sausage meat and perhaps a chicken liver or two, enlivened with seasoning, makes a splendid stuffing for a bird.

1. Sift the dry ingredients together into a mixing bowl.
2. Add the eggs and milk and beat with a wooden spoon.
3. Beat in the cream and lastly the melted butter.
4. Pour into an 22.5 × 28 cm (8½ × 11 inch) buttered cake tin and bake for 15–20 minutes in a preheated oven.
5. Cut into squares while still hot and serve wrapped in a cloth napkin.

ABOVE FAR RIGHT: Cornbread
RIGHT: Brown soda bread

BANANA BREAD

175 g (6 oz) sugar
100 g (4 oz) butter
2 eggs
2 tablespoons milk
225 g (8 oz) mashed ripe banana
225 g (8 oz) self-raising flour
2 teaspoons baking powder
1 teaspoon salt
100 g (4 oz) chopped walnuts

Preparation time: about 10 minutes
Cooking time: 1 hour
Oven: 180°C, 350°F, Gas Mark 4

My eldest child made this banana bread – and ate it enthusiastically, substantiating one of my arguments for getting children interested in cooking, which is that they will always at least try the things they have made.

This is a useful recipe to have at hand when bananas begin to grow too brown and spotty. They are, as you know, immensely nutritious, easily digestible and high in vitamins and minerals.

1. Cream together the sugar and butter. Beat in the eggs and the milk.
2. Fold in the bananas, which you have mashed slightly but not so much as to remove all texture from the loaf.
3. In another bowl sift together the dry ingredients and mix in the nuts.
4. Blend the dry mixture into the creamy one.
5. Bake in a greased loaf tin 23 × 13 × 7.5 cm (9 × 5 × 3 inch) in a preheated oven for 1 hour. Test with a skewer to see if done and, if the skewer comes out tacky, cook a little longer.

BRANDY SNAPS

100 g (4 oz) butter
100 g (4oz) caster sugar
120 ml (4 fl oz) golden syrup
100 g (4 oz) plain flour (sifted)
½ teaspoon ground ginger

Preparation time: about 10 minutes
Cooking time: about 15–20 minutes
Oven: 190°C, 375°F, Gas Mark 5

1. In the top pan of a double boiler, heat together the butter, sugar and syrup over simmering water until all is melted. Remove from the heat and stir in the flour gradually. Add the ginger and stir again.
2. Oil two baking sheets. Spoon small rounds of mixture on to one baking sheet, spacing well apart. Put in the oven.
3. Five minutes later, put in the second baking sheet. Five minutes later check the first sheet and if the mixture has spread into lace mats, is bubbling and a deep golden brown, remove it.
4. When the biscuits seem to solidify but are still bendy, roll them round the handle of an oiled wooden spoon. Slide them off and rest on a wire tray. Continue alternating the sheets until all cooked.

HEIDI'S COOKIES

4 tablespoons vegetable oil
75 g (3 oz) butter
75 g (3 oz) caster sugar
75 g (3 oz) brown sugar
1 egg
1 teaspoon vanilla essence
200 g (7 oz) self-raising flour
½ teaspoon bicarbonate of soda
½ teaspoon salt
100 g (4 oz) shelled walnuts, chopped
175 g (6 oz) plain chocolate chips

Preparation time: 15 minutes
Cooking time: 15–20 minutes
Oven: 190°C, 375°F, Gas Mark 5

This recipe, given to me by an American acquaintance, is quick and easy to make and goes down as a treat with children. Once bitten, the cookies are likely to be made by the children themselves. The mixture is not a million miles away from a brownie recipe and the result should have a similar stickiness. Also like brownies, the mixture puffs up in the oven and then sinks upon cooling, but don't let this alarm you – it is the correct procedure.

1. Cream together the oil, butter and two sugars. Beat in the egg and vanilla.
2. Sift together the self-raising flour, bicarbonate of soda and salt.
3. Stir the flour into the mixture, add the walnuts and the chocolate chips and blend them in fairly evenly.
4. Spread the mixture in a 33 × 24.5 cm (13 × 9½ inch) baking tin. Cook in a preheated oven for 15–20 minutes until the surface is puffy.
5. Let cool and then cut into squares.

ABOVE LEFT: Banana bread
LEFT: Brandy snaps
BELOW LEFT: Heidi's cookies

OATCAKES

25 g (1 oz) lard, dripping or bacon fat
300 ml (½ pint) hot water
450 g (1 lb) medium oatmeal – extra for the rolling
½ teaspoon bicarbonate of soda
½ teaspoon salt

Preparation time: 10 minutes
Cooking time: 20 minutes
Oven: 150°C, 300°F, Gas Mark 2

1. Melt your chosen fat (bacon fat is good) in the hot water.
2. In a bowl mix the oatmeal with the bicarbonate of soda and salt.
3. Make a well, pour in the melted fat and water and mix with a knife to a fairly moist dough.
4. Dust a surface with oatmeal and roll out the dough, using plenty of oatmeal to prevent any sticking.
5. Cut into rounds and bake for about 20 minutes on an ungreased baking sheet in a preheated oven, turning several times, until they are crisp.

WATER BISCUITS

225 g (8 oz) plain flour
1 teaspoon baking powder
½ teaspoon salt
50 g (2 oz) butter or margarine
sea salt
poppy seeds, or sesame seeds or caraway seeds (depending on the cheeses that will accompany)

Preparation time: 5 minutes
Cooking time: 20 minutes
Oven: 150°C, 300°F, Gas Mark 2

1. Sift together the flour, baking powder and ½ teaspoon salt. Rub in the fat and add enough water to make a firm dough.
2. Roll out thinly on a floured surface. Prick all over with a fork and cut out circles with a cup or biscuit cutter.
3. Sprinkle just with sea salt or with your choice of seeds as well.
4. Bake on a lightly oiled sheet in a preheated oven for about 20 minutes.
5. If you store them, crisp in a low oven when you need them.

EGGIE'S BISCUITS

100 g (4 oz) hard margarine, not butter
100 g (4 oz) caster sugar
1 dessertspoon milk
1 dessertspoon golden syrup
175 g (6 oz) plain flour
1 teaspoon bicarbonate of soda
50 g (2 oz) bran flakes

Preparation time: about 10 minutes
Cooking time: 15 minutes
Oven: 190°C, 375°F, Gas Mark 5

1. Cream together the margarine and sugar. Add the milk and syrup.
2. Mix together the sifted flour and bicarbonate of soda and stir into the mixture.
3. Fold in the bran flakes. Roll heaped teaspoons of the mixture into walnut-sized balls.
4. Place quite far apart on greased baking sheets and bake in a preheated oven for 15 minutes. Cool on a wire rack.

ABOVE RIGHT: Oatcakes and waterbiscuits
BELOW RIGHT: Eggie's biscuits

RECIPE AND MENU PLANNER

SPRING DINNER PARTY

Confucius salad: page 20

Baked whole salmon: page 56

Rhubarb fool: page 114

SUMMER DINNER PARTY

Grilled goat's cheese with salad: page 19

Raie au beurre noir: page 52

Clafoutis: page 144

AUTUMN DINNER PARTY

Fried aubergines with skordalia: page 12

Duck breasts with apple: page 69

Pecan pie: page 110

WINTER DINNER PARTY

Palestine soup: page 12

Quails with interesting rice: page 70

Tarte Tatin: page 106

FAMILY SUPPERS

Designer pizza: page 27

Fresh fruit

Eggs Lucullus: page 31

Plum crusts: page 110

Corned beef hash: page 78

Blackberry and apple crumble: page 113

Authentic Caesar salad: page 100

Salt-grilled hamburger: page 82

VEGETARIAN SUPPERS

Cheese fondue: page 28

Stir-fried vegetables with curried omelette: page 103

Potage bonne femme: page 8

Pasta with fresh tomatoes and basil: page 36

Stuffed mushrooms: page 19

Risi e bisi: page 40

Celeriac remoulade with anchovy toasts: page 20

Croûtons omelette: page 32

FOOD FACTS

HELEN DORE

FAST FOOD

TIME SAVERS

Nothing gives more pleasure and satisfaction than serving good food to family and friends. But today even the keenest cooks find that the time they can actually afford to spend in the kitchen is often strictly limited. Combining a job with running a home, looking after children (a full-time job if ever there was one!), not to mention all kinds of voluntary and leisure activities, all take up a surprising number of hours in the day. So in most households meals need to arrive on the table fast, but this doesn't mean you have to be down at the takeaway every night, or spend vast sums on expensive ready-prepared foods or made-up dishes from the supermarket. Instead, follow the tips and know-how given in this section to help you beat the kitchen clock when you're late home from the office, when friends drop in unexpectedly – whenever, in fact, you need to produce a meal at short notice. You'll find that the recipes in this book, all of which can be prepared and cooked within an hour (sometimes with some advance preparation) offer a wealth of fast food ideas for every occasion, from a simple family supper to the smartest dinner party. The Recipe and Menu Planner on page 124 gives a handy breakdown of fast meals for a variety of occasions.

FAST FOOD FACTS

Planning: the fastest cooks have invariably got advance planning down to a fine art. It doesn't take more than a few minutes to sit down and plan a week's meals, but this can make all the difference to your timetable later on, saving you literally hours of precious time during the week, helping you to shop sensibly – and, of course, to produce really well-balanced meals, Plan your work, too, whenever you cook a dish. Well-written recipes like the ones in this book show in the method how to make the most economic use of time, but you can do a lot to help yourself too here: read the recipe in advance, make sure you have all the ingredients you will need, and get them out ready to use, along with whatever equipment is required. This is how all the best chefs work, with incredibly speedy results. So get the planning habit – it really does save a lot of time.

Shopping: once you've got your menu plan for the week worked out, draw up a shopping list of all the ingredients you know you will need. With this to refer to, you can save so much time in the shops. Aim to do most of your week's shopping in one go and try to choose a time when supermarket queues are short – avoid Friday evenings and Saturday mornings if you can! Popping out to the shops every day can be a time-consuming – and expensive – activity, so try to shop ahead just once a week and top up in between with only perishable items like milk, fish, salads, etc.

Store cupboard: a really well and imaginatively stocked store cupboard can be a real time saver in so many ways. (You'll find some useful hints for store-cupboard standbys on page 128.) Make a note of essentials such as sugar, oil, etc., as they run low, and, when you're shopping, don't forget to buy long-life store-cupboard items as well as the ingredients you need for immediate use. It's well worth keeping an eye open for special offers on tinned foods at your local supermarket, as there are often real bargains to be had.

Advance preparation: if you find yourself with an hour or two to spare, use this effectively to help you save time when you need it most. For example, preparing a quiche from scratch can be quite a lengthy process, but takes no time at all if you've got a pre-baked pastry case ready to be filled and popped into the oven. Below you will find suggestions for all sorts of basic advance preparations.

Batch-cooking: get into the habit of making two or more dishes in the time it takes to prepare one! Soups, stocks, sauces, casseroles, pastry and cakes, as well as many other dishes, can very usefully be made in batches.

Freezer: even a small freezer can make all the difference when time is at a premium. Use it to freeze away batch-cooked dishes in handy serving quantities, and to store useful staples like frozen pastry, vegetables and ice cream and sorbet for instant desserts. Remember that clear labelling of foods for the freezer is a great help.

Microwave: this high-speed cooking method is the ultimate time-saver – every busy cook should have a microwave oven! It will cook all kinds of foods in a fraction of the time required by the conventional method and will make short work of jobs like making jam or marmalade which you thought you'd never have time for! A microwave will also defrost food in minutes, saving hours on thawing time. And, because in the microwave food is cooked in special containers which can often be used as serving dishes as well, there's another real time-saving when it comes to doing the washing up.
Fan-assisted oven: in this special type of conventional oven, a fan element circulates the heat over, around and underneath the food and cuts down dramatically on cooking time – by as much as a third.
Food processors, mixers and blenders: a food processor or electric mixer can prove invaluable in making short work of all sorts of time-consuming, fiddly jobs, like creaming cake mixtures, kneading bread doughs, chopping and grating vegetables, and so on. If you are cooking for large numbers in a hurry, a food processor is undoubtedly a boon. However, a simple blender can also be put to a surprising number of uses, such as making bread crumbs, grinding nuts and spices, chopping herbs, etc.
Kitchen design: a professionally designed and fitted kitchen doesn't just look good, it saves on time and labour simultaneously. Even if you don't have the very latest in kitchen design, try to ensure that you have plenty of worktop space; that the contents of the cupboards are arranged so that equipment you use every day is readily accessible; that you can easily transfer food from worktop to cooker and from cooker to sink without having to walk the full length of the kitchen; and that there are no awkward spaces between units where debris can accumulate.
Fast-cooking foods: go for foods that cook naturally fast, like fish, offal, mince, pasta, eggs, green vegetables, etc. If you like to cook your own pulses, choose quick-cooking ones like split lentils. See pages 136-7.
Fast cooking methods: develop a range of techniques suited to cooking specially fast: stir-frying, steaming, grilling, flash-frying, etc., rather than casseroling, roasting, etc. You will find more about these methods on pages 136-40.
Short-cuts: by all means make good use of the time- and labour-saving prepared foods available in increasing variety from supermarkets. Ready-scrubbed potatoes, trimmed and cleaned leeks, cauliflower trimmed and broken into florets, interesting selections of salad leaves, etc., are becoming as increasingly familiar as sliced bread and are just as convenient! But do remember that it's the convenience you are paying for, and that these foods can work out quite expensive.
No-cook food: this is, of course, the fastest food of all! Salads make delicious starters as well as main courses and accompaniments; super-quick dips and chilled soups, like gazpacho and avocado, can be whizzed up in seconds in a blender, and an interesting cheeseboard and selection of fresh fruit can be just as welcome as the most elaborate, time-consuming pudding. As with all fast food, the key to success is in clever shopping: explore your local delicatessen for goodies like real Italian salami and other spicy continental sausages, raw Parma ham, marinated herring fillets and unusual cheeses, etc.; treat yourself to some of the exciting exotic fruits like pawpaw, passion fruit, mangos and star fruit that are now increasingly available, and use all these to help you produce delicious meals fast.

STORE-CUPBOARD STANDBYS

Depending on the size of your cupboard, any/all of the following would be very useful to help speed up your cooking.

TINNED FISH

Sardines: these are available canned in oil or tomato sauce. Mash them with lemon juice for an instant pâté and serve garnished with lemon wedges, accompanied by hot toast.
Tuna: available in oil or brine (less fattening). Combine drained flaked tuna with canned butter beans and thinly sliced onion for an authentic Italian starter, or with salad leaves, sliced cucumber, etc. as a quick and easy main course. Tuna mashed with mayonnaise makes a popular sandwich filling.
Anchovies: very good in a sauce to serve with fish or pasta, as a garnish for pizza and salade niçoise, or mixed with scrambled eggs.

TINNED VEGETABLES

Tomatoes: peeled whole or chopped Italian plum tomatoes are one of the most useful store-cupboard items. They are excellent as the base of an infinite number of pasta sauces.
Petits pois: cooked in the French style with tiny pearl onions, these are really delicious, with a very sweet flavour. They are certainly worthy of serving as a vegetable accompaniment in their own right. Look for those labelled 'extra fine' as these are the tiniest peas of all.
Canned pimientos: very useful for quick curried dishes, as the fresh ones are quite fiddly and time-consuming to prepare.
Ratatouille: this vegetable stew, full of Mediterranean flavour, makes a tasty accompaniment to baked fish or chicken breasts.
Artichoke hearts: very good to give a touch of luxury to a salad or pizza topping, or serve them as part of a mixed hors d'oeuvre.
Sweetcorn: kernels are useful for soups and salads, or for adding to vegetable mixtures. Baby sweetcorn are good in stir-fries, particularly in authentic Chinese stir-fried vegetables.
Potatoes: new potatoes, especially Jersey Royals, are worth keeping in store for emergencies. Serve them hot, tossed in butter with some chopped mint, or cold in a quick potato salad.

OTHER TINNED GOODS

Soups: Gourmet soups such as game, or lobster or crab bisque, are good enough for any first course, served with some crunchy croutons. Tinned consomme – beef or chicken – can be very useful in making quick sauces.
Tinned fruit
Peaches (especially white peaches), apricots, pears, pineapple rings, guava and lychees are useful as the basis for a fruit salad. Buy fruit tinned in natural juice rather than sugar syrup, which can be very sickly.

OIL AND VINEGAR

Olive oil: use a good-quality virgin oil, from the first pressing, whenever a rich, fruity flavour is required.
Sunflower oil: being virtually tasteless, is an ideal multi-purpose oil.
Nut Oils such as walnut or hazlenut give a subtle flavouring to salad dressings.
Wine vinegar is the most useful all-purpose vinegar.
Flavoured vinegars lend instant interest to sauces and dressings. Various herbs – garlic, black peppercorns and raspberries – are just some of the flavourings used.

SAUCES AND FLAVOURINGS

Soy sauce: available dark and light. Use in stir-fried dishes and in marinades.
Worcestershire sauce: lends spiciness to hamburgers, meat loaves, shepherds pie and scrambled eggs – not just to tomato juice!
Tomato ketchup: useful ingredient in a quick sweet and sour sauce.
Sun-dried tomatoes: packed in olive oil, these have a wonderfully warm Mediterranean flavour and are much more interesting than tomato purée or ordinary canned tomatoes.

Pesto: a jar of this delicious Italian sauce made of basil, pine nuts, cheese and olive oil has a number of uses. It is traditionally served with pasta, but is also very good stirred into chunky vegetable soups or spooned over baked potatoes.
Mustards: keep a choice of smooth, creamy Dijon, hot English mustard, and a good whole-grain mustard and use to give sparkiness to sauces, dressings, etc.
Mayonnaise: keep a good-quality thick bottled mayonnaise, storing it in the refrigerator once it is opened.
Redcurrant jelly: a useful quick glaze for fruit tarts, as well as a serving accompaniment. Combine it with port, citrus juice and rind to make Cumberland sauce. Delicious with ham, tongue and poultry.
Horseradish sauce: the traditional accompaniment to roast beef, but also delicious with smoked fish, to make a no-cook starter or simple main course.
Dried herbs: are nowhere like as good as fresh, but dried oregano in particular has a number of uses, especially to flavour pizza and pasta sauces.
Stock cubes: are, of course, extremely quick to use, but not really recommended; not only do they have a high monosodium glutamate content, which many people find unacceptable on health grounds, they also tend to give a very uniform taste to food. Continental vegetable stock cubes are best and may be obtained from delicatessens and shops supplying kosher foods.
Dried mushrooms: dehydrated Italian porcini or Japanese shiitake mushrooms give a wonderful flavour to soups, stocks, sauces, risottos, omelettes, etc. They are quickly reconstituted by soaking in warm water.
Salt: sea salt ground in a salt mill is best for both cooking and table use. Flavoured salts, such as garlic, onion or celery, can also be useful in fast cooking.
Pepper: freshly ground pepper makes all the difference to the way food tastes. Try experimenting with green and pink peppercorns as well as black.
Spices: whole spices you grind yourself are well worth the little extra time this takes. Whole nutmeg and cinnamon sticks, and a vanilla pod which you can bury in a jar of sugar for instant vanilla-flavoured sugar, are some of the most useful standby spices.

GRAINS

Rice: long-grain basmati rice and Italian medium-grain risotto rice (arborio) are both especially quick-cooking types.
Couscous: processed from semolina and pre-cooked, is a virtually instant food. It is extremely good in stuffing mixtures, or lightly steamed to serve as an accompaniment.
Bulgur wheat: or cracked wheat is ready to use after only brief soaking; it requires no cooking and is the principal ingredient, combined with lots of chopped parsley and mint, fruity oil and sharp lemon juice, in the delicious Middle Eastern salad, tabbouleh.

DRIED PASTA

Keep a variety of shapes for different uses. Don't forget that pasta can be used to make delicious, substantial and unusual salads.

BREADS AND BISCUITS

Wafer-thin melba toast, available in packets, is ideal with pâtés and other starters, as are **grissini,** Italian bread sticks. Crispbreads and toasts are also useful store-cupboard standbys; miniature toasts are ideal for quick canapes to serve with drinks.

FREEZER STANDBYS

Apart from all the dishes you can cook ahead and freeze to save time, the following are a selection of the commercially frozen products for which it is well worth making freezer space.
Pastry: buy shortcrust and puff pastry in 225 g /8 oz and 450 g /1 lb sizes to cater for different recipe requirements. Phyllo pastry, sometimes referred to as strudel leaves, is extremely useful and freezes just as well as the other pastries: use it to make savoury nibbles in interesting shapes to serve with drinks or as a starter, or to wrap round quick-cooking lamb cutlets or chicken breast fillets. Vol au vent cases are another useful freezer standby: tiny ones filled with an interesting mixture and served hot are excellent at a drinks party; larger vol au vents with a chicken or prawn filling make a nice supper dish.
Vegetables: there is a vast selection of frozen vegetables to choose from. Among the most useful are leaf or chopped spinach, petits pois, broad beans and sweetcorn.
Chopped herbs: these freeze very well and can be added frozen to hot sauces, soups, etc., to give instant flavour.
Kipper fillets: useful for quick starter pâtés.
Chicken livers: make a delicious pasta sauce as well as rich pâté.
Peeled prawns: handy for use in starters, salads, canapes, sandwiches, sauces, etc.

FAST FLANS

A savoury flan makes a very popular supper dish, with a large mixed salad, or a welcome starter if you are serving a light main course. Keep a supply of pastry cases in the freezer, then just fill and bake. This way, preparation and cooking will take well under 1 hour.

Rub the fat into the flour

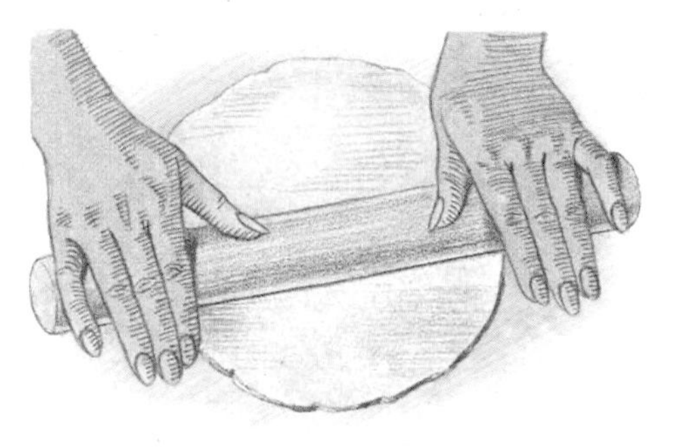

Roll out pastry to a circle

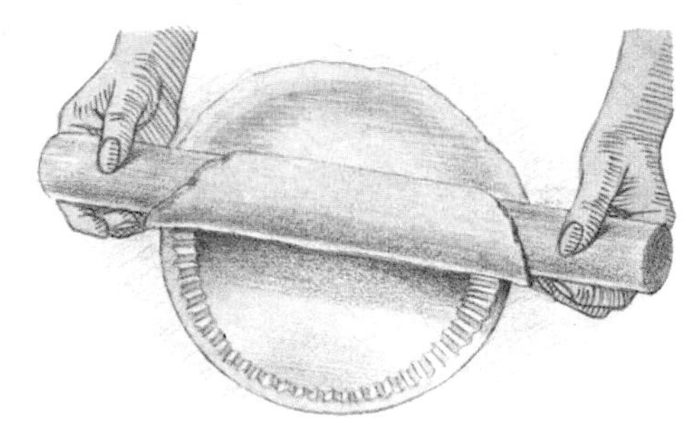

Drape the pastry over the flan case

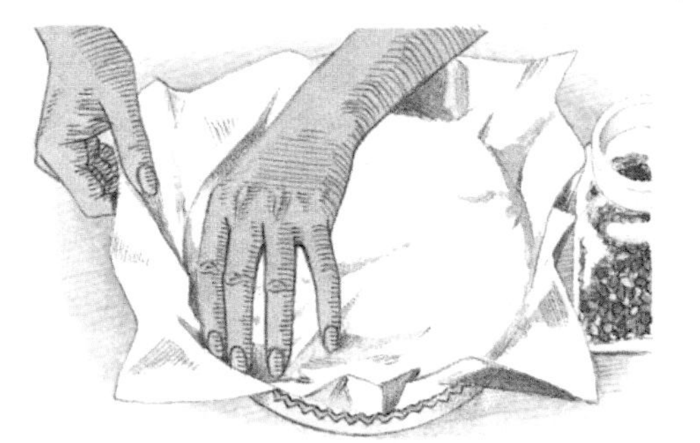

Line with greaseproof paper to bake blind

FREEZING PASTRY

Pastry freezes very well, either raw or baked.

Freezer life
Unbaked pastry: 3 months
Baked pastry: 6 months

Pastry dough: make a good quantity of pastry and freeze in handy amounts, e.g. 225 g/8 oz; 450 g/1 lb. Allow 2–3 hours for thawing at room temperature so that the pastry rolls out easily and does not crumble.

Pastry cases: these may be frozen raw or baked blind before freezing (see below). Use foil flan cases for lining with pastry, or use flan tins lined with foil which may be removed after open-freezing. Open-freeze until solid, then stack the flan cases with discs of waxed paper between each, wrap in foil, pack in a rigid container for extra protection, and freeze. Remove the wrapping while the pastry is frozen, then thaw for 1 hour at room temperature before filling, or fill and bake from frozen, allowing 10–15 minutes extra baking time.

FLAN PASTRY

Shortcrust is the best pastry for flans. The basic recipe given here uses 225 g/ 8 oz flour. Vary the ingredients in proportion according to the flan size you require.

FLAN SIZES

Flan case	**Flour**
15 cm/6 inch	100 g/4 oz
18 cm/7 inch	150 g/5 oz
20 cm/8 inch	175 g/6 oz
23 cm/9 inch	200 g/7 oz
25 cm/10 inch	225 g/8 oz

SHORTCRUST

225 g/8 oz plain flour
a pinch of salt
50 g/2 oz butter
50 g/2 oz lard or white vegetable fat
a little iced water

1. Sift the flour with the salt into a mixing bowl. Cut the fats into the flour, using a round-bladed knife.
2. Using the fingertips, lightly rub the fat into the flour, until the mixture has the consistency of breadcrumbs. Lift the mixture high into the air as you work, to incorporate as much air as possible.
3. Using the knife, gradually mix in just enough iced water to make the pastry adhere. Shape lightly into a ball.
4. If freezing the dough at this stage, shape into a rectangular block, as lightly and quickly as possible, then wrap in polythene or foil and seal securely.
5. If using the dough immediately, cover and allow to rest in the refrigerator for 30 minutes before rolling out.

MAKING PASTRY IN A FOOD PROCESSOR

A food processor makes excellent pastry fast, and is especially useful for large quantities.

- Using the metal blade, cut the fat into the sifted flour and salt in the bowl, at high speed and in short bursts.
- Stop processing immediately the mixture looks like breadcrumbs, or the pastry will be tough and difficult to handle.
- When adding the liquid through the funnel, stop processing immediately the mixture forms large lumps, before it comes together in a ball of dough.
- Turn out on to a lightly floured board or work surface and complete the kneading by hand, to give an extra light pastry.

SHORTCRUST PASTRY VARIATIONS

Cheese: add 3 tablespoons finely grated Cheddar and 1 tablespoon grated Parmesan to the rubbed in mixture.
Herb: add 2 teaspoons dried herbs to the rubbed in mixture.
Wholemeal: use a half and half combination of plain wholemeal and white flours, for a nutty texture. You will need a little more water for mixing.
Egg-enriched: use an egg yolk beaten with a little iced water to mix the dough.
All-butter: use all butter instead of a mixture of fats, for an extra 'short' pastry.

LINING A FLAN CASE WITH PASTRY

1. Measure the depth of the flan case. Double this measurement and add it to the diameter of the case.
2. Roll out the pastry to a circle slightly larger than this measurement. Work on a lightly floured board or work surface, using a lightly floured rolling pin, and roll in the same direction, away from you, using short, light strokes.
3. Use the rolling pin to lift the pastry and drape it carefully over the flan case. Press the pastry gently into the base and sides, taking care not to stretch it. Trim off the excess pastry round the rim, using a sharp knife. Freeze raw or bake blind, as preferred.

BAKING A FLAN CASE BLIND

This prevents the pastry base from rising up and the sides from collapsing during baking. It also prevents the pastry from becoming soggy once the filling is added.

1. Prick the pastry base all over with a fork.
2. Line the pastry with a piece of greaseproof paper or foil cut 5 cm/2 inches larger than the case. Cover with baking beans or uncooked pulses, rice or short-cut macaroni, in an even layer.
3. Bake at 200 C/400 F/Gas Mark 6 for 15–20 minutes, then carefully remove the lining paper and beans. Return to the oven for 5 minutes to dry out.

FLAN FILLINGS

For a 25 cm/10 inch flan lined with pastry made with 225 g/8 oz flour, use 3 eggs whisked with 150 ml/¼ pint single cream and 150 ml/¼ pint milk as the savoury custard base. To this add:

- Finely shredded leeks and diced bacon, lightly fried
- Thinly sliced mushrooms, lightly fried and flavoured with ground coriander
- Sliced tomatoes with chopped basil
- Flaked tuna with sweetcorn
- Smoked salmon trimmings with dill
- Crabmeat seasoned with cayenne pepper
- Lightly steamed broccoli florets, with grated Cheddar cheese
- Crumbled Stilton
- Asparagus tips with grated Gruyère cheese
- Spinach flavoured with nutmeg

BAKING FLANS

1. Preheat the oven to 180 C/350 F/Gas Mark 4.
2. Place the filled flan on a baking sheet and bake in the centre of the oven for 30–50 minutes, depending on size, until the pastry is browned and the filling set. Allow 10–15 minutes extra if baking from frozen.

FAST PANCAKES

Pancakes are delightfully versatile. They can be made sweet or savoury, rolled up round a filling, or stacked up with a choice of fillings between the layers and served cut into wedges like a cake. They are popular with children and are equally good as a starter or main course. Best of all, they freeze very well, either flat or filled and rolled. Used from the freezer pancakes become one of the fastest foods.

Freezer life
Unfilled pancakes: 4 months
Filled pancakes: up to 2 months

BASIC PANCAKE BATTER
MAKES 12 PANCAKES

100 g/4 oz plain flour
a pinch of salt
1 egg
1 egg yolk
300 ml/½ pint milk
1 tablespoon melted butter

Good news for cooks in a hurry – this batter may be used immediately and does not require standing. It may be made extra quickly in a food processor.

1. To make the batter by hand, sift the flour with the salt into a mixing bowl and make a well in the centre. Beat the egg with the egg yolk and pour into the well.
2. Using a wooden spoon, gradually draw the liquid into the flour, slowly adding half the milk from a jug, to make the batter smooth. Gradually stir in the remaining milk and the butter.
3. If using a food processor, sift the flour with the salt into the bowl. Add the egg and egg yolk and blend, then blend in the milk added in a steady stream. Finally blend in the melted butter.

FRYING PANCAKES

1. Heat a crêpe pan, rub with a piece of paper towel dipped in tasteless vegetable oil, such as sunflower, and heat again.

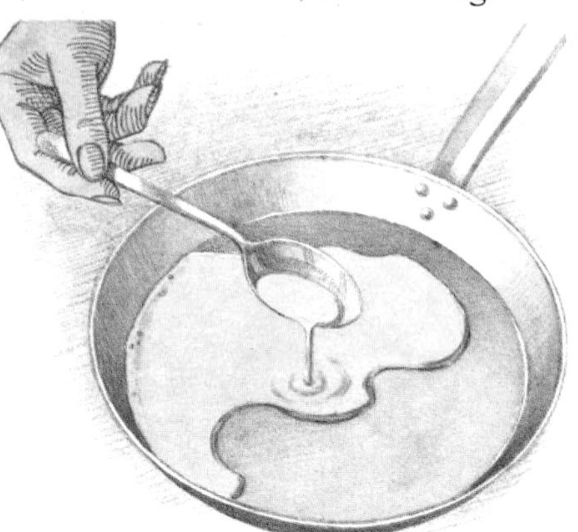

Add the batter to the crêpe pan

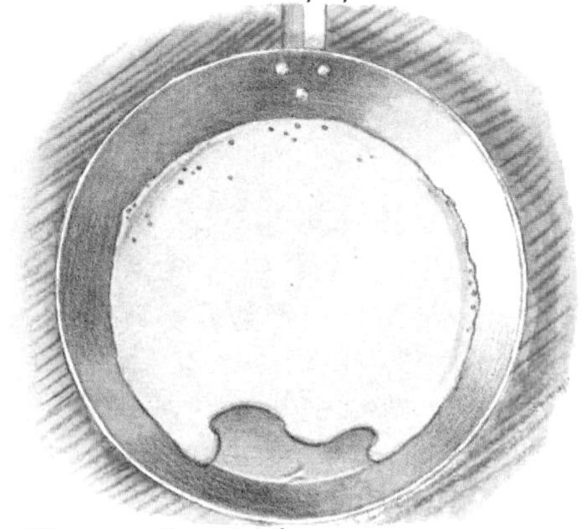

Tilt pan so the entire base is covered

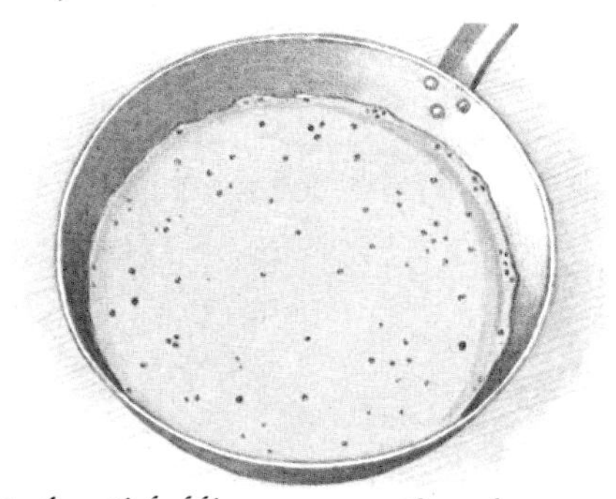

Cook until bubbles appear on the surface

2. Add 2 tablespoons pancake batter to the pan, tilting the pan evenly so that the entire base is covered.
3. Cook until bubbles appear on the surface and the underside is browned, then turn the pancake, using a fish slice, and cook briefly on the other side. Slide on to a plate and make the remaining pancakes in the same way, greasing the pan with more oil as necessary, and stacking up the pancakes as they are made, with a piece of greaseproof paper between each.

FILLING PANCAKES

Filling suggestions

- Mushrooms in soured cream
- Chopped spinach and ricotta cheese
- Seafood, such as prawns and mussels, in a thick tomato or white wine sauce
- Smoked haddock in béchamel sauce
- Cooked chicken, mushrooms and bean sprouts in a little béchamel
- Diced ham with puréed sweetcorn
- Ratatouille
- Puréed avocado
- Well-reduced bolognese sauce made with best-quality minced beef and chicken livers

For rolled pancakes: lay the pancake flat on a work surface. Spoon the filling towards one end of the pancake, about 1 cm/½ inch from the edge. Roll up. Place the pancakes in a single layer in an ovenproof dish. Sprinkle with grated cheese and place in a moderate oven for about 20 minutes, until the cheese is melted and bubbling.

For stacked pancakes: place a pancake flat on a lightly greased baking sheet. Spread with the filling of your choice. Top with another pancake and continue layering, alternating the fillings, if liked, until you have a stack of 6 pancakes. Sprinkle the top with grated cheese and heat through in a moderate oven for about 20 minutes, until the cheese is melted and bubbling. Serve cut into wedges.

SWEET PANCAKE IDEAS

- Sweeten the basic batter with 1 tablespoon caster sugar
- Add the finely grated rind of 1 small orange or lemon to the batter
- Replace 15g/½ oz of the flour with 1 tablespoon cocoa powder
- Use fruit juice or liqueur to replace some of the liquid
- For apple pancakes, fill with puréed apple flavoured with cloves or cinnamon
- For Black Forest pancakes, fill with drained tinned black cherries mixed with fromage frais
- For apricot pancakes, fill with thick purée made with dried apricots
- Serve rolled sweet pancakes dredged with icing sugar or with scoops of ice cream
- Serve sweet pancakes plain, sprinkled with lemon juice and caster sugar
- Or fold pancakes into quarters, to make triangles, and heat through in a mixture of 75 g/3 oz butter, 85 ml/3 fl oz orange liqueur, 85 ml/3 fl oz fresh orange juice, 4 tablespoons caster sugar, then flame with brandy.

FREEZING PANCAKES

Unfilled pancakes: open-freeze individually, then interleave with discs of waxed paper and freeze in a stack, wrapped in foil. To thaw, remove the wrapping and separate the individual pancakes. Leave for 20 minutes at room temperature.
Filled pancakes: open-freeze until solid, then pack in a rigid container. Reheat from frozen in a moderate oven.

FAST TIPS

Salad dressing

A good vinaigrette dressing transforms the simplest salad into something special. This dressing keeps so well in a screwtop jar in the refrigerator that it is well worth making in quantity, to save yourself time. The amounts given in the following recipe will dress at least 4 large salads. The basic mixture may be varied by the addition of chopped fresh herbs, crushed garlic, finely chopped shallot, etc.

salt and freshly ground black pepper
2 teaspoons Dijon mustard
1 teaspoon sugar
4 tablespoons white wine vinegar or lemon juice
12 tablespoons olive, walnut or sunflower oil

Dissolve salt and pepper to taste, the mustard and sugar in the vinegar or lemon juice in a bowl or jug. Gradually whisk in the oil until the mixture is thoroughly blended. Check the seasoning, then pour into a screwtop jar. Store in the refrigerator and shake well before use.

Herb ice cubes

Fresh herbs enhance food wonderfully, but chopping them can be time-consuming. Instead, chop herbs in quantity in a food processor, then freeze them in ice cube trays, to lend instant, flavour to sauces, casseroles, etc. Once frozen solid, remove them from the trays and pack in bags to store in the freezer. Keep clearly labelled.

Breadcrumbs

Breadcrumbs have a variety of uses. For the fast cook, they are invaluable for coating quick-fried veal escalopes, fish fillets, chicken breasts, etc. As breadcrumbs will keep fresh for some time if stored in a jar with a tight-fitting lid in the refrigerator, it is well worth making good use of stale ends of bread in this way. Simply whizz to crumbs in a blender or food processor.

Grated cheese

Grated cheese is so useful in gratins, sauces, pizza toppings, etc., that it is an excellent idea to have a ready-grated supply to hand. Pack into small rigid containers and freeze.

DELI DISHES

Some of the fastest and tastiest main dishes and snacks can be put together in minutes using ready-cooked meat, smoked fish, unusual cheeses, interesting tinned foods, etc., from delicatessen shops. Many supermarkets now have well-stocked delicatessen counters, and it is well worth investigating these if you're short of time. All you need is a little imagination to put delicatessen foods to good use in the kitchen.

Mozzarella, tomato and avocado salad
To serve 2, cut 1 mozzarella cheese, preferably Italian, into thin slices. Skin and slice 2 large tomatoes. Peel, stone and quarter 1 small avocado and cut each quarter in half lengthways. Arrange the mozzarella, tomato and avocado slices on individual serving plates, alternating the ingredients and fanning them out from the centre of the plates. Drizzle over a little fruity olive oil, sprinkle with chopped basil and season well with coarsely ground black pepper. Serve with grissini (Italian bread sticks).

Parma ham with fruit
Wafer-thin slices of raw Parma ham combined with slices of fresh fruit make the quickest and most delicious of starters. Melon is traditional with Parma ham, but it is rewarding to experiment with other fruits as well: sliced mango, paw paw or peaches, and quartered fresh figs are all excellent.

Tongue rolls
For a quick, easy summer lunch, spread slices of cooked tongue thickly with cream cheese or quark flavoured with chives and chopped capers or gherkins. Serve the tongue rolls on a bed of assorted salad leaves.

Herring salad
Roll mop herrings are delicious with a mixture of diced potato, beetroot and apple, topped with a swirl of soured cream. Serve as a starter or with a selection of salads as a main course.

Salami and pasta salad
Cook some fresh spinach tagliatelle noodles, drain and while still hot toss in a well-flavoured vinaigrette dressing (see page 133). Cut some best quality Italian salami into strips and combine with the pasta. Sprinkle with parsley and garnish with tomato wedges.

Smoked mackerel with apple horseradish
Combine equal quantities of horseradish cream and apple purée (apple sauce in a tin or jar may be used) and serve with smoked mackerel fillets, as a starter or light main course.

Avocado with taramasalata
Simply spoon taramasalata into halved and stoned avocado pears and serve with wholemeal bread and butter as an easy and original first course.

Pastrami open sandwich
For a tasty snack or light lunch dish, spread slices of rye bread with butter, then Dijon mustard. Cover with slices of pastrami and top with sliced gherkins.

Hummus
Drain a 425 g/15 oz can of chickpeas, reserving 5 tablespoons of the liquid. Put the chickpeas and reserved liquid into a blender with 1 crushed garlic clove, 1 tablespoon lemon juice, 1 tablespoon tahini paste and 1 tablespoon olive oil. Blend to a smooth purée. Taste and add more lemon juice and oil, if required, and season well with salt and pepper. Spoon into a bowl, sprinkle with a little olive oil and paprika pepper, and serve as a dip. Or spread in pitta bread with coleslaw as a healthy and substantial lunchtime snack. Hummus freezes well: to use from the freezer, allow to thaw completely, then beat until smooth.

Jellied consomme with soured cream and caviare
Chill a tin of beef consomme, then spoon into individual serving dishes. Top each serving with a swirl of soured cream, sprinkle with snipped chives and add a teaspoon of red or black lumpfish roe.

Pear with blue cheese dressing
In a blender, process 75 g/3 oz Danish Blue cheese with 2 tablespoons each of thick yoghurt and mayonnaise until smooth and creamy. Thin down, if necessary, with a little cream. Halve, core and peel a large pear, place cut side down on individual plates and spoon over the dressing.

Assemble the ingredients for tapenade

Gradually add the olive oil

Use as a dip with crudités

Greek salad
Combine cubed Feta cheese with diced cucumber, chopped spring onion, wedges of tomato and shredded crisp lettuce. Dress with vinaigrette, scatter over a few black olives and some chopped coriander or parsley, and serve as a starter, with some hummus, taramasalata and warm pitta bread, or as a side salad.

Artichoke heart, bean and pasta salad
Combine drained tinned artichoke hearts, sliced with lightly cooked broad beans popped out of their skins, and cooked pasta shells (green if possible), and toss in a herb vinaigrette. Serve as a starter or side salad, or add strips of cooked or Parma ham for a light main course.

Smoked trout pâté
In a blender or food processor combine 75 g/3 oz each of soft butter and curd cheese, then add the juice of 1 small lemon, 1 teaspoon finely grated lemon rind and 350 g/12 oz flaked smoked trout fillets. Process until smooth, then season with freshly ground black pepper and pack into ramekin dishes. Chill for 2–3 hours and serve with melba toast. This is also good made with kipper fillets.

Tapenade
In a blender or food processor process 1 can anchovy fillets, drained, 100 g/4 oz pitted black olives, 1 tablespoon capers, 1 teaspoon each of Dijon mustard and lemon juice, 1 tablespoon brandy and ¼ teaspoon freshly ground black pepper. When smooth, gradually blend in 3 tablespoons olive oil, until thoroughly combined. Use by itself as a dip with crudités, or combined with mayonnaise as a dip or sauce for eggs and fish.

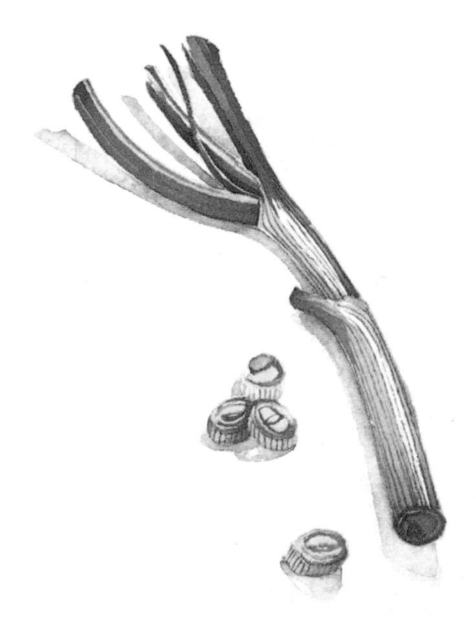

FOOD PROCESSOR MENUS

A food processor copes at lightning speed with many time-consuming kitchen jobs. Mayonnaise and crème patissière, useful and versatile basic preparations, can be made successfully in a food processor.

Gradually add the olive oil

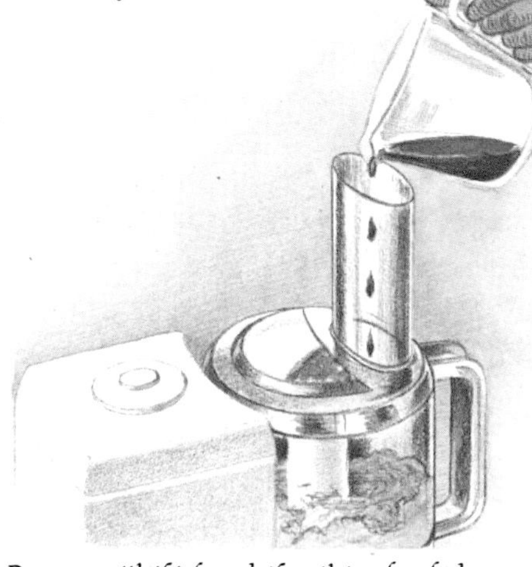

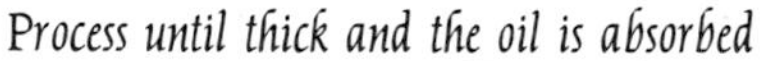

Process until thick and the oil is absorbed

MAYONNAISE

2 egg yolks
2 teaspoons Dijon mustard
300 ml/½ pint olive oil
1 tablespoon wine vinegar
salt and pepper

1. Fit the food processor with a plastic blade, which has a gentler action than the metal chopping blade, and is more suitable for blending delicate mixtures.
2. Place the egg yolks, mustard and 1 tablespoon oil in the processor and process for 5 seconds. Dribble the remaining oil through the feed tube with the motor running. Switch off the motor once all the oil has been amalgamated and the mayonnaise is thick.
3. Add the vinegar, with salt and pepper to taste, and process again for 3 seconds.

CRÈME PATISSIÈRE

50 g/2 oz caster sugar
3 egg yolks
2 tablespoons plain flour
2 tablespoons cornflour
300 ml/½ pint milk
few drops of vanilla essence

1. Fit the food processor with the metal chopping blade. Place the sugar and egg yolks in the processor bowl and process until pale. Add the flour and cornflour and process for a few seconds.
2. Bring the milk to the boil and immediately add to the bowl while the motor is running.
3. Transfer the mixture to a heavy saucepan and heat, stirring constantly, until thickened. Beat in the vanilla essence and leave to cool. Use as a filling for choux buns and fruit flans and tartlets.

WINTER SUPPER MENU

French onion soup
•
Lamb patties
Coleslaw
•
Apricot fool

QUICK FRENCH ONION SOUP

450 g/1 lb onions
50 g/2 oz butter
425 g/15 oz can beef consomme
450 ml/¾ pint water
1 tablespoon beef extract
4 slices French bread
75 g/3 oz Cheddar cheese, grated
3 tablespoons brandy

The food processor really comes into its own here as it takes over the task of slicing a large quantity of onions for this speedy version of a classic onion soup.

1. Fit the food processor with the slicing disc and slice the onions.
2. Melt the butter in a large saucepan, add the onions and fry until a rich brown. Add the consomme, water and beef extract and bring to simmering point.
3. Toast the French bread on both sides and top with the grated cheese. Toast until the cheese is bubbling.
4. Stir the brandy into the hot soup and ladle into individual soup bowls. Float a cheese toast on the top of each bowl.

LAMB PATTIES

225 g/8 oz couscous
450 g/1 lb boneless lamb, cubed
1 onion
1 teaspoon ground cinnamon
salt and pepper
vegetable oil for basting

1. Soak the couscous in cold water for 1 hour. Strain well.
2. Fit the metal chopping blade and chop the lamb and onion very finely. Mix with the wheat, add the cinnamon and season to taste with salt and pepper. Process in batches until smooth.
3. Shape into 12 flat patties. Brush them with oil and cook under a preheated moderate grill for 5 minutes on each side.

COLESLAW WITH PEPPERS

175 g/6 oz red cabbage
1 small green pepper
1 small red pepper
1 small onion
salt and pepper
6 tablespoons mayonnaise (see page 136)

1. Fit the food processor with the slicing disc and slice the cabbage. Cut the peppers in half lengthways, remove the seeds, then slice.
2. Slice the onion or chop coarsely, using the metal chopping blade.
3. Place the vegetables in a salad bowl and season to taste with salt and pepper. Add the mayonnaise and stir well to combine.

APRICOT FOOL

225 g/8 oz dried apricots, soaked overnight in 450 ml/¾ pint water
75 g/3 oz caster sugar
300 ml/½ pint double cream
1 egg white

1. Simmer the apricots with their soaking water for 15–20 minutes, until softened. Drain, reserving the liquid.
2. Process to a purée, adding a little of the cooking liquid if the purée seems very stiff.
3. Stir the sugar into the purée. Whisk the cream until it forms soft peaks and fold into the purée. Whisk the egg white until stiff but not dry and fold this in also. Spoon into glasses to serve.

SUMMER DINNER PARTY

Chilled Beetroot Soup

•

Halibut with Julienne of Vegetables

•

Raspberry Millefeuille

CHILLED BEETROOT SOUP

350 g/12 oz cooked beetroot
150 ml/¼ pint soured cream
600 ml/1 pint chicken stock
salt and pepper
snipped chives to garnish

1. Put the beetroot and half the cream in the processor bowl and process until smooth. Transfer to a bowl and stir in the chicken stock. Season to taste with salt and pepper. Chill well.
2. Pour into individual soup bowls and swirl the remaining cream on top of each bowl. Sprinkle with chives.

HALIBUT WITH JULIENNE OF VEGETABLES

4 halibut steaks
vegetable oil for brushing
salt and pepper
2 carrots
1 leek
2 celery sticks
50 g/2 oz butter
2 tablespoons lemon juice

1. Brush the halibut steaks on both sides with oil. Season well. Place under a preheated moderate grill and grill for 5–6 minutes on each side, until tender. Transfer to a warmed serving dish.
2. Meanwhile fit the food processor with the grating disc, or julienne disc if you have one. Shred the vegetables.
3. Melt the butter in a frying pan, add the vegetables and fry gently until soft. Add the lemon juice and simmer for 2 minutes. Spoon over the halibut to serve.

RASPBERRY MILLEFEUILLE

225 g/8 oz frozen puff pastry, thawed
1 quantity crème patissière (page 136)
225 g/8 oz raspberries
icing sugar, to finish

1. Preheat the oven to 220 C/425 F/Gas Mark 7.
2. Roll the puff pastry out thinly and cut into 2 equal-sized rectangles. Trim the edges neatly with a sharp knife. Place the pastry rectangles on a moistened baking sheet.
3. Bake in the oven for about 15 minutes or until puffed up and golden. Using a fish slice, transfer to a wire rack to cool.
4. Split each pastry rectangle into 2 horizontally. Spread a layer of crème patissière on 3 of the rectangles, sprinkle each with raspberries and layer up. Top with the remaining piece of pastry, press down lightly and sprinkle with sifted icing sugar.

FAST FOOD IN THE MICROWAVE

Owning a microwave oven means that you can easily give a midweek supper party, even if you're out at work all day and are really pushed for time. Amazingly, the three-course menu for 4 given here involves a total of only 1 hour's preparation and cooking time. Make life even easier for yourself by preparing the starter and dessert the night before, and serve a salad with the main course, or a dish of the vegetables that cook so well in the microwave: 450 g/1 lb broccoli, for example, broken into small florets, will cook to perfection in 8 minutes on HIGH.

MICROWAVE MENU
Chicken liver pâté
•
Trout with anchovy stuffing
•
Caramelized oranges

CHICKEN LIVER PÂTÉ

225 g/8 oz chicken livers, trimmed and chopped
100 g/4 oz streaky bacon rashers, rinded and chopped
1 onion, thinly sliced
1 tablespoon wholegrain mustard
1 tablespoon brandy or sherry
1 garlic clove, crushed
100 g/4 oz soft butter
salt
freshly ground black pepper
lemon slices and parsley sprigs, to garnish

1. Place the livers, bacon and onion in a 1.75 litre /3 pint microwave-proof dish with the mustard, brandy or sherry and garlic.
2. Cover with microwave film and microwave on HIGH for 4 minutes. Stir well, then cover again and microwave on HIGH for a further 4 minutes until tender. Allow to cool.
3. Purée the mixture in a blender or food processor with the butter until smooth. Season to taste with salt and pepper.
4. Spoon into ramekin dishes and chill for at least 1 hour before serving, garnished with lemon slices and parsley sprigs. Accompany with melba toast or fingers of hot toast.

TROUT WITH ANCHOVY STUFFING

25 g/1 oz butter
2 shallots, or 4 spring onions, finely chopped
75 g/3 oz fresh breadcrumbs
4 anchovy fillets, finely chopped
2 tablespoons chopped parsley
finely grated rind and juice of 1 lemon
freshly ground pepper and salt
4 whole trout, about 300 g/11 oz each, cleaned

1. Put the butter into a medium ovenproof glass bowl and microwave on HIGH for 1 minute until melted. Stir in the shallots or onions, cover with microwave film, pulling back one corner to allow steam to escape, and microwave on HIGH for 5–7 minutes until the shallots or onions are softened. Stir in the breadcrumbs, anchovies, parsley, lemon rind and juice and season to taste with pepper and a little salt.
2. Fill the trout cavities with the stuffing mixture, then slash the skin twice on each side. Place the trout side by side in

Make diagonal slashes in the trout skin

a large microwave proof dish.
3. Cover with microwave film, pulling back one corner and microwave on HIGH for 8–10 minutes until cooked, turning the trout over and repositioning halfway during cooking. Allow to stand for 5 minutes before serving accompanied by cucumber sauce (page 140).

CARAMELIZED ORANGES

8 medium oranges
225 g/8 oz caster sugar
2 tablespoons curaçao or other orange liqueur

The microwave makes easy work of preparing caramel, and there are no sticky pans to cope with.

1. Thinly pare the rind from 2 of the oranges, taking care not to remove any of the pith. Cut the rind into very thin strips.
2. Peel the remaining oranges and remove the pith from all of them. Slice the oranges into rounds and remove the pips. Arrange the slices overlapping in a serving dish.
3. Put 6 tablespoons water into a microwave proof dish and microwave on HIGH until boiling, then add the sugar and stir until dissolved.
4. Microwave the sugar syrup on HIGH for 5–6 minutes until it turns a golden caramel colour. Immediately pour on 200 ml/7 fl oz boiling water. Add the strips of orange rind and microwave on HIGH for 4–5 minutes until the orange rind is tender and the caramel dissolved.
5. Remove from the oven and stir in the liqueur. Leave to stand for 10 minutes, then pour over the orange slices and chill for at least 1 hour.

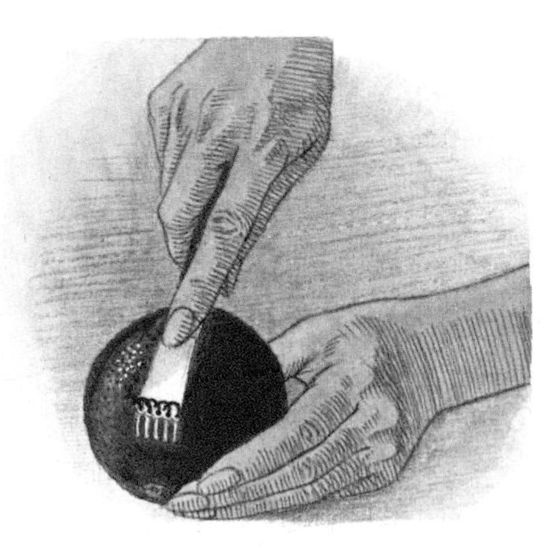

Pare the rind with a lemon zester

Add sugar to boiling water and stir

Add orange strips to the caramel sauce

MICROWAVE SAUCES

When you're in a hurry and have to cook fast, sauces are usually the last thing you imagine there'll be time for. However, quick sauces are a speciality of the microwave – lump-free, creamy and velvet-textured, with no risk of scorched saucepans. Here is a useful savoury and sweet selection.

BÉCHAMEL SAUCE

300 ml/½ pint creamy milk
1 bay leaf
6 black peppercorns
1 blade mace
1 small onion, peeled
1 clove
1 small carrot, peeled and halved lengthways
25 g/1 oz butter
2 tablespoons plain flour
½ teaspoon salt

1. Pour the milk into a 900 ml/1½ pint microwave proof bowl. Add the bay leaf, peppercorns, mace, onion stuck with the clove and the carrot. Microwave uncovered for 2 minutes on HIGH, then cover and leave to infuse for 10 minutes.
2. Put the butter into a 900 ml/1½ pint heatproof measuring jug. Microwave, loosely covered, on HIGH for 30 seconds. Stir in the flour and microwave on HIGH for 20 seconds.
3. Strain the infused milk into the roux, whisking constantly. Add the salt and microwave on HIGH for 3 minutes, uncovered, whisking at 1-minute intervals. Whisk well after removing from the microwave.

FRESH TOMATO SAUCE

450 g/1 lb ripe tomatoes, chopped
1 onion, chopped
1 tablespoon olive oil
1 tablespoon wine vinegar
1 teaspoon soft brown sugar
1 bay leaf
1 teaspoon chopped fresh thyme or basil
salt and freshly ground black pepper

This sauce freezes well. Use it as a pasta or pizza sauce, or to layer the stacked pancakes on page 133.

1. Reduce the tomatoes and onion to a purée in a blender, food processor or vegetable mill.
2. Put the purée with the remaining ingredients in a microwave proof dish, cover with a lid or microwave film and microwave on HIGH for 3 minutes, stirring from the edges to the centre halfway during cooking.
3. Taste and adjust the seasoning and discard the bay leaf.

CUCUMBER SAUCE

1 large cucumber
50 g/2 oz butter
1 teaspoon plain flour
1 tablespoon white wine vinegar
150 ml/¼ pint fish stock or water
2 teaspoons finely chopped tarragon
salt and white pepper

This goes extremely well with fish.

1. Using a potato peeler, thinly peel the cucumber. Cut in half lengthways and scoop out the seeds with a teaspoon. Finely chop the flesh.
2. Put the butter into a large ovenproof glass bowl and microwave on HIGH for 1 minute until melted.
3. Stir the chopped cucumber into the butter and cover the bowl with microwave film, pulling back one corner. Microwave on HIGH for 6 minutes until very soft, stirring two or three times.
4. Blend the flour with the vinegar and stir in the stock or water. Stir the mixture into the cucumber and stir in the tarragon. Microwave on HIGH for 3–4 minutes until boiling, stirring frequently. Season to taste with salt and pepper.

BARBECUE SAUCE

50 g /2 oz butter
1 large onion, finely chopped
1 garlic clove, crushed
1 tablespoon tomato ketchup
2 tablespoons wine vinegar
2 tablespoons demerara sugar
2 teaspoons mustard powder
¼ teaspoon chilli powder
2 tablespoons Worcestershire sauce

1. Put the butter into a medium ovenproof glass bowl and microwave on HIGH for 1 minute until melted.
2. Stir the onion and garlic into the melted butter, cover the bowl with microwave film, pulling back one corner, and microwave on HIGH for 5–6 minutes until softened.
3. Whisk all the remaining ingredients together with 150 ml/¼ pint water and stir them into the onion. Microwave on HIGH for 5 minutes, stirring frequently.

CHOCOLATE FUDGE SAUCE

5 tablespoons single cream
25 g/1 oz cocoa powder
100 g/4 oz caster sugar
175 g/6 oz golden syrup
25 g/1 oz butter
pinch of salt
½ teaspoon vanilla essence

Delicious poured over ice cream and very popular with children.

1. Combine all the ingredients except the vanilla in a medium ovenproof glass bowl and stir well to mix.
2. Three-quarters cover with microwave film and microwave on HIGH for 5 minutes until boiling, stirring frequently.
3. Stir in the vanilla and allow the sauce to cool slightly before serving.

APPLE SAUCE

450 g/1 lb Bramley cooking apples, peeled, quartered, cored and sliced.
juice of 1 lemon
2 tablespoons caster sugar
25 g/1 oz soft butter

Another sauce that is specially useful for the freezer. Serve with pork or duck.

1. Put the apples, lemon juice and sugar into a 2.75 litre /5 pint ovenproof glass bowl. Cover with microwave film, pulling back the corner, and microwave on HIGH for 5–6 minutes until the apples are soft, stirring several times.
2. Purée the mixture in a blender or food processor. Beat in the butter.

Turn back a corner of the microwave film

INDEX

ACKNOWLEDGEMENTS

Photography

HOWARD ALLMAN

Photographic Styling

MARIAN PRICE

Preparation of food for photography

ANNE HILDYARD AND LYN RUTHERFORD

Illustrations

DELYTH JONES

Step-by-step illustrations

PATRICIA CAPON

Cover photograph

VERNON MORGAN

Preparation of food for cover photography

ALLYSON BIRCH